RAGE

Gerry Smith

WORK RAGE

Identify the Problems
Implement the Solutions

HarperBusiness
HarperCollins*PublishersLtd*

WORK RAGE:
IDENTIFY THE PROBLEMS, IMPLEMENT THE SOLUTIONS
Copyright © 2000 by Gerry Smith.
All rights reserved. No part of this book may be used or reproduced
in any manner whatsoever without prior written permission
except in the case of brief quotations embodied in reviews.
For information address HarperCollins Publishers Ltd,
55 Avenue Road, Suite 2900, Toronto, Ontario,
Canada M5R 3L2.

http://www.harpercanada.com

HarperCollins books may be purchased for educational,
business, or sales promotional use. For information please write:
Special Markets Department, HarperCollins Canada,
55 Avenue Road, Suite 2900, Toronto, Ontario,
Canada M5R 3L2.

First edition

Canadian Cataloguing in Publication Data

Smith, Gerry, 1956–
Work rage:
identify the problems, implement the solutions

ISBN 0-00-638549-4

1.Violence in the workplace.
I. Title.

HF5549.5.E43S64 2000   658.3'8   C99-932229-X

00 01 02 03 04 HC 6 5 4 3 2 1

Printed and bound in the United States

Contents

November 1999, Seattle. A stranger walks into a building in a harbor-front shipyard office and begins shooting people he encounters. Two men die and two are seriously wounded.

November 1999, Hawaii. A disgruntled, about-to-be-fired employee goes on a shooting rampage at a Xerox plant where he had worked for 10 years. He kills seven of his colleagues.

July 1999, Atlanta. A man fairly new to the stock trading world kills his wife on Tuesday, his children on Wednesday, and shoots 21 trading colleagues at two brokerage firms on Thursday, nine of whom die. He had recently accumulated losses on the market. It was reported that he had been the main suspect in the murder of his former wife and mother-in-law in 1993.

April 1999, Taber, Alberta. A 14-year-old boy walks into his local high school and shoots two teenage fellow students. One, a 17-year-old, dies; the other is wounded.

April 1999, Littleton, Colorado. Two teenagers go into Columbine High School and start spraying bullets everywhere. Thirteen people are killed. The two boys commit suicide.

April 1999, Ottawa. A former disgruntled employee of O.C. Transpo enters the workplace with a gun and shoots his former colleagues. Four are killed, two wounded and he commits suicide.

Introduction

About 12 years ago, while I was in the last throes of making a momentous decision to leave the Catholic priesthood, a friend of mine asked me the question that eventually prompted me to write this book about rage in the workplace.

I can remember, after what had been a pleasant dinner, sitting in Eddie's living room in Scotland, overlooking the beautiful River Clyde just at the point where it joined the Holy Loch. It was sunset. The sunlight disappearing over the hilltops and shimmering on the river was breathtaking. Out of the blue my friend, a man in his early sixties, a well-traveled retired IBM executive, asked me, *What are you going to do about violence?*

The question floored me. Conversations with Eddie were always philosophical, deep, sometimes religious in nature. We had previously discussed the seemingly more visible signs of violence, not just in the community where we lived, but in a more general way around the world. However, I wasn't sure how to answer such a personal question. *What was I going to do about violence?*

After years of being haunted by Eddie's somewhat prophetic question, I have reached a point in my career when it makes sense that I do, in fact, "do" something about violence. This book, therefore, is my contribution—my answer to that question posed to me all those years ago.

If you are a reader looking for an academic treatise on the origin and development of the violent response in humans, this book will not be for you. The intention is not to question the nature of rage, but to propose some ways to prevent violence or lessen its impact. In particular, I want to share my own experience, some of which may be useful for others concerned about creating safe work environments.

It will become clearer to the reader as we proceed that I do not intend to concentrate on violence in the home. Much interesting research has already been accomplished in the area of domestic abuse. Rather, I want to share some of the more recent experiences of the past 10 years, during which I have worked in the field of employee assistance, and in particular the past five years, during which I have worked in *trauma response*. In that capacity, I have been providing help and support to victims and witnesses, both employees and their families, affected by rage or violence in the workplace.

By way of introduction, then, I would like to say a few

words about my career. Like many people, I now do for a living something I never envisioned doing 25 years ago when I first entered university. From a very early age in life—I don't know exactly when—I had decided that I wanted to be a doctor or a priest. I recall that upon discovering that priests could not marry, I decided to stay away from the priesthood. The idea of not being able to marry did not seem too appealing to my young mind at that time. But as the years passed and my interest in the Church grew, so too did the idea of becoming a priest become more appealing. So I went off to seminary at a young age, studied in Rome for seven years at a pontifical university, and emerged as a fully ordained Catholic priest, ready to take up the duties and responsibilities of an assistant priest back in my native Scotland.

From day one, I realized that I had made a big mistake. Yes, I was extremely good at doing the "job"—ministering to the sick and the dying, marrying young, enthusiastic couples and carrying out all the social functions associated with the church in a local community. Since I had been trained in counseling at university, being the "therapist" became a large part of my active ministry. But something was not working for me: the priesthood, I knew, was meant to be more than a "job." The title "Father Gerry" never really rang true for me, for lots of reasons (and that will probably lead to another book someday). I tried at various times during those first years to "get out," but it wasn't easy. I'm sure there were times when my family wondered what was going on with me.

I couldn't bring myself to tell them that I didn't actually like being The Priest.

After eight years and three different assignments, I took the plunge and left behind the security of the Church to make my own way. My decision to move was complex. I had experienced these three assignments, had worked under three different bosses, and had eventually been my own boss at the end. Still being discontent even running my own household, I knew that it was not just the living arrangements of life in the priesthood that were not suitable for me. I had other and perhaps more serious issues with Church dogma, especially around divorce and remarriage, sexuality, contraception and, of course, celibacy.

On leaving, I took a stop-gap job at Marks and Spencer for a few months while I sought advice and counsel about the direction of my future career. It became clear to me that my counseling skills were my strongest attribute, and so I sought work in an area where those skills would be best utilized. I joined the world of *employee assistance* and began working as a full-time counselor, first in Glasgow, Scotland, and later in Toronto, Canada, my adopted nation. Throughout almost 10 years with the Church, and another 10 in employee assistance, responding to the effects or impact of violence on people has played a significant part in my day-to-day work life.

As a priest, my introduction to the world of violence came early, during my first week in a new parish. Being the "rookie"—yes, there are rookie priests, too—I was "on call." If a call for pastoral help came in during the night, I was the one who had to get out of bed to provide the support of the Church to whomever was requesting aid. In my first ever on-call experience, I was awakened by the telephone at an ungodly hour—if you'll excuse the pun—of two or three in the morning. The call, if I remember correctly, came from a policeman asking me to rush to a house in the parish neighborhood where a homicide had taken place.

Being new to the area, I asked for directions and was informed that the home was in the Strone, a neighborhood that I had already been informed was infamous for drug and alcohol abuse, moneylenders, crime and high unemployment. It was a socially deprived neighborhood, the likes of which exist in many cities throughout the world. (As an aside, I was subsequently to become a "friend" of one of the leading moneylenders in this same neighborhood, who truly believed she was providing a social service to the poor residents!)

Hurrying on foot, I followed the directions to the house, to discover on arriving that there had been a domestic dispute. I was brought up to speed quickly by the police. Mr. and Mrs. McNab had been drinking heavily. A fierce argument broke out. Mrs. McNab became so enraged that she picked up a large kitchen knife and lunged at her husband, attempting to stab him in the chest. Being inebriated at this point, she staggered and missed, but when she fell, the knife plunged into Mr.

McNab's arm, "accidentally" severing an artery. He bled to death before help arrived.

Could I now provide help to Mrs. McNab's ailing elderly mother, who was currently wailing in one of the bedrooms?

This really was not a scenario for which I was prepared: a dead body, blood everywhere, an arrested wife, a wailing mother, and screaming traumatized children and neighbors. Seminary did not train a priest for this. I was ready with the Holy Oils, prepared to say the prayers for the dead and comfort the living. But all I remember feeling was a profound sense of shock, as though I were having a nightmare.

A reality check, however, told me that this was not the time for pious platitudes and mumbled prayers. The counselor in me came out, and in what seemed like second nature, I started the process of what I later came to know as "trauma debriefing" for the old lady wailing in bed and for the assembled neighbors and family. I asked them about what had happened, where they had been when it happened, how they had heard, what they were thinking, and how they were feeling at this early stage. This was my swift introduction to violence, rage and the surrounding chaotic impact.

As a postscript to the Strone story, weeks and months passed by after the homicide, and more information became known to me and to the entire community. Mr. and Mrs. McNab had been married for almost 20 years, during which she had been admitted to hospital more than 22 times with broken bones, cuts and other husband-induced injuries. She had been a constant victim of what we now refer to as "domestic abuse." Yet when judgment day eventually came, she was tried in court and given two years' probation for her "crime." The last time I heard of her, about 15 years ago, she still lived in the Strone and was slowly rebuilding her shattered life.

Thankfully, over the years rage has seldom been directed at me (or by me!). It has not affected me personally, except in terms of what professionals describe as "vicarious traumatization"—a danger in the therapy world. It occurs when an innocent bystander or listener to a story (for example, a counselor) can be almost as badly affected as if they had been involved in the incident from the outset.

Still, both my career paths have led me to deal with rage and its effects, and I know the time is now ripe to share my experiences with other people who are trying to make a difference. I can recall numerous horrific incidents, and will use some of them as examples in *Work Rage* to demonstrate my own particular growth in awareness of the problems associated with violence, and my growth in responsiveness to people affected by the rage of others.

When I think today about my old friend Eddie, I recall being wined and dined handsomely, watching the sun set slowly over the beautiful Scottish landscape. And then I recall being stunned into serious thought about an area that has now become an increasingly serious problem in the developed world. It is my sincere hope that some of you, in reading this book, will be encouraged to give more thought to the issue of workplace violence, and will learn a better way to deal with the frustrations and bitter arguments that can escalate into work rage.

Chapter 1

Rage Defined

I think, sometimes, that I know what rage feels like.

When I was in grade seven at school, I remember picking a fight with the boy in my class who was considered to be the toughest in the school—a bit of a school bully! We were in the middle of the school soccer field, and a large group of kids had congregated quickly when they heard the chant "Fight! Fight! Fight!" I have no idea what the fight was over. I just remember the fact that I instigated it. That in itself was unusual. I wasn't really known as a fighter—in fact, quite the opposite. I was a quiet kid.

I remember being scared stupid at the throw of the first punch, and I knew I did not have a hope in hell of even hurting him. But I really felt the need to punch, kick and throttle the living daylights out of him. And that's what happened. We punched, kicked and grabbed each other around the neck. The blows came one after another, and with the blows the pain. It was obvious that I was totally outmatched, but I was determined I was not going to give up. Eventually, the teacher on yard duty caught sight of us and rushed over to break us up. We were marched off to the Headmaster's office, where we both received a dose of The Strap, six of the best across the open palms with a large, thick leather-belt-like instrument, the standard form of corporal punishment used in the school at that time. Afterwards, we were both sent home.

On the way home—a short walk of about 10 minutes for me—I remember feeling absolutely exhilarated. I was hurting all over, but I felt so proud of myself for tackling a bully. It was a good, satisfying feeling. And, needless to say, I did not have any trouble with him again. In fact, shortly afterwards, we both became altar boys in the local church. When I look back at that fight, I think of how stupid I was, acting on the spur of the moment like a prize bull, knowing my chances of success were zero. Being angry, and acting it out in that schoolyard way felt good. It makes me wonder if the sensation I had then is similar to what people feel today when rage takes over and they lash out, physically or verbally.

The rage of a youngster, however, is different from the rage of an adult. The young person is still learning, still differentiating between right and wrong, still mastering the art of control. An adult, in our determination, is one who knows right from wrong, who has control and mastery of self. The rage that demonstrates itself in the workplace in a way reflects the rage of the schoolyard: the immature, highly charged lashing out at another in a variety of ways, including verbal, physical, and emotional or psychological. But the difference lies in the fact that we have a higher expectation of the mature individual: mature behavior. Work rage cannot and should not be tolerated in any way, shape or form.

Is Canada a safe place to live? We are told constantly by the press and by politicians eager to gain one more vote that Canada is among the world's best places to live. Who would want to argue with that? Certainly not I, who have made my home here in recent years like so many others wishing to partake of opportunity and the great Canadian way of life. However, in my recent years, as a person who responds to tragedy on behalf of many organizations throughout Canada, I have begun to wonder. Is this country as safe as we would all like to believe?

To earn my bread and butter, I head up the National Trauma Response Service for a company called Warren Shepell Consultants. Twenty years ago, Warren Shepell, a visionary entrepreneur, started offering psychological consulting services to corporations that wished to provide counseling support to employees facing difficulties in life that could affect their work performance. Thus, *employee assistance programs*, or *EAPs*, were born in Canada.

Part of the range of services available to the companies who use Warren Shepell and other EAPs is psychological support in the event of tragic events or disaster. It's sad to say, but this is a growing business. At one time, the Trauma Response service was infrequently used by companies, but today—as a result of increased societal pressures to provide victim support and growing awareness of the fallout associated with being involved in a traumatic event—it has become highly desired by many small and large organizations.

When I began working with Warren almost six years ago, the Trauma Department serviced about 15 to 20 events every month. Today, the figure is closer to 80 or 90. Not only have the number of interventions increased, but the type and severity of incidents has become more acute. A typical day in the department used to find my colleagues and me arranging support for people affected by a bank robbery in the morning and then, perhaps, a workplace death in the afternoon. Nowadays, we might begin the day by supporting victims of a colleague's suicide, followed by an incident of workplace rage, then a horrific accident on the 401 (Southwestern Ontario's major highway), and finally an ugly murder/suicide.

My function within the department is to oversee the response to these events—to ensure that the appropriate type of help is provided at the right time to the right people. It also falls to me to recognize trends within the "trauma business." A dedicated team of colleagues develops new methods to respond to tragedy, and we train the many counseling staff who work the length and breadth of the country using different therapies to alleviate the effects of traumatic stress on the victims of disasters, small and large. Trends are not always easy to identify, especially in the absence of reliable statistics. We have been lucky in recent years to build up useful data banks, and we are finally becoming able, in this computer age, to analyze the trends. From this vantage point, I can point to an increase in the number of traumatic events caused by rage in the workplace.

When I first started responding to trauma, there were only ever a few incidents every month relating to workplace violence. Today such incidents amount to more than 30 percent of our total workload. The service responds to more than 1,000 events every year—more than 300 of them related in one way or another to violence or rage in the workplace. The reasons for this— some of which I will attempt to expand upon later in this book—are varied and complex.

Note that the Trauma Response Service we provide is like a "mop-up." The damage is already done; we go in to deal with the aftermath. The situations we respond to are usually very serious. It stands to reason that if the number of serious incidents is on the rise—as our figures indicate, and as I truly believe—then logic dictates that the number of minor ones is also on the rise. So I return to my question at the beginning of the chapter: Is Canada a safe place to live?

The International Labor Organization in Geneva, Switzerland, would also have us question the safety of the Canadian workplace. This organization has in recent years been outstanding in carrying out worldwide surveys on workplace trends for employees. A 1998 report indicated that even the United States is a safer place than Canada for female employees. In fact, one can deduce from their in-depth investigation that for every woman in the U.S. who suffers a physical assault in the workplace, there will be four assaulted in the Canadian workplace. That figure may be shocking, especially given our penchant for belittling our American neighbors for their "violent" society.

PREVALENCE OF VICTIMIZATION AT THE WORKPLACE BY TYPE OF INCIDENT, GENDER, REGION AND COUNTRY, 1996 (percentages)

Region/Country	Assault		Sexual Incidents, Female only
	Male	Female	
Western Europe	3.6	3.6	7.0
Austria	0.0	0.8	0.8
England & Wales	3.2	6.3	8.6
Northern Ireland	2.3	3.7	6.0
Scotland	3.1	2.6	6.2
Finland	3.1	4.3	6.6
France	11.2	8.9	19.8
Netherlands	3.6	3.8	7.6
Sweden	1.7	1.7	3.5
Switzerland	4.3	1.6	4.8
Countries in transition	2.0	1.4	3.0
Albania	0.4	0.4	0.8
Czech Republic	1.9	0.8	2.3
Georgia	1.7	0.9	2.1

Hungary	0.6	0.0	0.5
Kyrgyzstan	2.5	3.4	5.3
Latvia	1.0	0.8	1.5
Macedonia (former Yugoslav Republic of)	0.8	0.5	1.4
Mongolia	1.4	1.6	2.8
Poland	0.9	1.3	1.9
Romania	8.7	4.1	10.8
Russian Federation	0.4	0.5	0.9
Yugoslavia (Federal Republic)	3.2	2.4	5.8
North America	**2.5**	**4.6**	**7.5**
Canada	3.9	5.0	9.7
United States	1.0	4.2	5.3
Latin America	**1.9**	**3.6**	**5.2**
Argentina	6.1	11.8	16.6
Bolivia	0.4	0.9	1.3
Brazil	0.2	0.4	0.8
Costa Rica	0.8	1.4	2.2
Asia	**0.4**	**1.0**	**1.3**
Indonesia	0.3	1.1	1.5
Philippines	0.5	0.8	1.0
Africa	**2.3**	**1.9**	**3.7**
South Africa	0.7	0.7	1.3
Uganda	3.2	4.3	7.2
Zimbabwe	3.0	0.7	2.6

Source: International Crime (Victim) Survey, 1996.

We know for a fact that workplace homicide in the U.S. is a major problem, there being at least three workplace homicides every day of the year. Not so in Canada. Even in my short experience as a member of the Canadian workforce, as someone who takes an avid interest in these kinds of statistics, and as someone who provides support in cases of workplace violence, I know that homicide is not a regular occurrence at work in Canada. Over the past six years, I have encountered only a handful of workplace homicides. Here in Canada, such deaths are such an unusual occurrence that they make national news; incidents that have come to my notice, or in which I have been involved professionally, have all been given national coverage. However, for reasons of discretion and confidentiality, I will be mentioning few of them by name in this book.

So homicide is not a problem—but what about all the other acts that we would define as "violent"? Assaults, verbal attacks, racial slurs, overbearing controlling bosses—where do these fit into the equation?

Over the years, for obvious reasons, I have become quite opinionated about rage and violence. But then, almost everyone has something to say on the subject. For example, most people can remember bosses who have been abusive, or parents who have been hot-tempered, or children who have been labeled as "problem children" because of their propensity to hurt others in the schoolyard. Yet, would we be quick to describe the people in these situations as violent? Are they exhibiting violence or rage? This is a difficult question.

When I think of the word *rage*, I often imagine a spontaneous outburst, an immediate and instantaneous reaction which is angry and hostile. I imagine that this reaction is short-lived and can be over and forgotten quickly. When I think of violence, I often jump to the horrific picture, the terrifying, fearful event that involves injury and harm, even death and destruction. The violent act is a product of rage, so I see the terms as being close in meaning, and throughout this work the words will be used interchangeably.

I remember a boss in my past who epitomized rage. He would get extremely angry, turn a deep purple-red, and develop the flared nostrils and glassy eyes. You could watch the build-up until he couldn't hold back any longer—and out would come a torrent of rage. Fortunately, it never came my way, but was usually directed at an innocent victim under his control, usually a nonassertive and fairly defenseless female office clerk who just happened to be in his way. (This boss was a former executive of a labor union who had "jumped the fence" and become a senior manager in a human resources department. I'm sure the tactic of aggression had been useful in his past, but it was hardly fitting for an HR manager. However, his suitability for the post is not my interest here.) What I want to highlight is that this man was full of the sudden, explosive features that the word *rage* conjures up for us. Whether or not he would actually become physically violent is not really the issue. And, as far as I know, he has not been known to assault anyone, physically. I sometimes think that we are likely to forgive an outburst of rage more quickly than we would forgive violence. But should we? What, exactly is the difference?

When I talk about *work rage*, let me be clear about what I mean to include and exclude. First, for different work situations, there may well be different inclusions and exclusions. Initially, work rage is any action, directed at a person or a situation, that demonstrates loss of physical, verbal or emotional control. This can take the form of something simple, such as malicious swearing, or it can be something severe, such as throwing a punch in a fit of temper. Both situations illustrate loss of control. Both are examples of rage. And both are typical scenarios found in any workplace. My question is: Do we find one okay and the other offensive? Is it okay to swear but not okay to punch someone with whom we have a day-to-day work relationship?

From the outset, I want to make it clear that I think neither is an acceptable workplace behavior. However, that said, where do we draw the line?

I myself have been known to use offensive language. I know, however, that I have never thrown a punch. But does that make me an okay person? Am I not still hurting someone even if all I'm doing is using offensive language? Of course I am.

In many ways I suppose what is acceptable in the workplace depends on what employers want to achieve during work hours. Is the worksite to be a place where the respect and dignity of every single person is honored?

I firmly believe that everyone has the right to respect. And respect, as I understand it, is not only the right to be free from discrimination and harassment, but the right to be free from fear and intimidation. Therefore, I believe every employer has a duty to make it clear to all his or her employees as to what is and what is not acceptable behavior at work. This means ensuring that every employer is able to define *violence* and *rage* for their particular environment. So when I return to my definition above—that rage is the absence of physical, verbal or emotional control—I find that clearly that definition is not explicit enough.

I hope that leaders in management and unions, human resources and occupational health will read this and use this template to initiate a process of creating a safer work environment for staff in their care. I define rage in the following way:

> Workplace rage is any physical assault, behavior considered to be threatening or abuse in a verbal manner that occurs in the work setting. It has to include, but is not limited to the following examples: beatings, stabbing, suicides and near-suicides, rapes and shootings. Rage also includes inducing psychological trauma through such means as obscene phone calls, threats and a presence of another person that can be considered intimidating. As well as this, the definition of

rage should include any type of harassment, such as being sworn at, shouted at or stalked.

Examples of Physical Assault

- Slapping
- Pinching
- Hair-pulling
- Spitting
- Tugging at clothing
- Biting
- Punching
- Kicking
- Scratching
- Sexual attack
- Shooting
- Suicide
- Throwing objects, such as food
- Deliberately damaging property
- Homicide

Examples of Verbal and Psychological Assault

- Swearing
- Shouting
- Obscene phone calls
- Racial slurs
- Veiled threats and open threats
- Declaration of intent to harm, now or later
- Gestures with the hands or other parts of the body
- Displays of any kind of weapon, or something resembling a weapon
- Intimidation of any kind

Chapter 2

Who Fits
the Profile?

"Watch out for the quiet ones."

Popular wisdom today suggests that the quiet person, or the loner, is the one of whom we should be wary. Is such a warning valid in the workplace? What characteristics, if any, predict who might exhibit rage? In recent years, we have seen an upsurge in the number of movies and TV programs in which the police, in order to catch the criminal, use the services of a "profiler," who assists the police in the identifying the criminals habits and behaviors. This is sometimes done by psychological means, as in the TV shows *The Profiler* and *Cracker*, and sometimes by almost psychic means, as in *Millennium*, and other shows, I'm sure, that I have not personally viewed. "Profiling" is in vogue, and I am sure that it can be an extremely valuable tool for TV producers and directors in their search for a way to boost ratings. (Despite my cynicism, I actually admire the large-sized Robbie Coltrane playing the role of the loud-mouthed, scotch-swilling always-in-trouble "Cracker," the psychologist/profiler from British TV Land.)

The real psychological science of profiling—decidedly more complex and less glamorous than that portrayed on TV—has an important part to play in the apprehension of criminals in our society. But we in the field have to be extremely careful, in talking about profiling, that we do not make it seem that it's as easy as picking items from a menu of ingredients that combine to create the potentially violent person. Profiling is not a simple process. It takes years of dedicated psychological research, of "pulling teeth," of dissecting and unraveling case histories, of drawing comparisons and similarities between offenders, of delving into the murkiest of waters, before a good psychologist can be considered an "expert." Nor is profiling an exact science, since it deals with the complexity of human personalities—and we all know from our own experience that no two people are ever truly the same.

Of course, we can point out physical likenesses among family members, and we can sometimes recognize habits and actions in ourselves that seem to be repetitions of behaviors we witnessed in our own parents—things we swore we would never do, but find ourselves doing anyway! But it is entering dangerous territory to say we can know for sure that because someone has most of the features of the violent person, he is a potentially violent person. A professional must have a great deal of certainty, experience, study and research, not to mention guts, to be in a position to certify someone as potentially violent.

Having said all that, it is still useful for all types of leaders, human resources staff and people involved in occupational health and safety in organizations to understand that there are certain features often shared by the kind of individual who may cause violence in the workplace. There is a place for using information widely available that will assist us in our tasks of making the workplace safer for all concerned. Profiling in and of itself is never going to be enough, but it is a first and necessary step in the right direction toward prevention education, and will, it is hoped, assist people who supervise others to be on the lookout for warning signs. As I have been known to say, and will surely say again, *Violence does not happen in a vacuum.*

The predictability factors are numerous and fairly complex—easy to understand, but hard to track within an organization where managers are not prepared or trained. Tracking of employees demands a hands-on style of supervision, which in these days of high staff-to-management ratios can be almost impossible to achieve. For example, a manager with 200 direct reports will find getting to know those staff to be an almost impossible task. That makes tracking behavior changes tricky.

I would like to highlight here that if an organization really wants to create a safe working environment, free from the threat of violent behavior, then people in positions of responsibility have to be able to get to know the staff who appear day after day to do their jobs. It is a must! One of the first prerequisites in creating a safe environment is to observe the "normal" behavior employees display in the work environment. Then, by observing changing behavior, managers and supervisors will be able to spot the subtle conflicts that begin to occur, and the quiet aggression that might build to a boiling point. In being aware of the small changes, managers can then take preventive steps to dissipate growing rage. Knowing the background profile of the potentially violent person should heighten this awareness, and give the managers impetus to act first, rather than waiting to see what happens.

So what about this profile? The more significant elements are the following:

Gender

Generally speaking, the violent person in our society is *male*. In the course of my working career I have seldom encountered violent situations where the perpetrator is female. Obviously, there are occasional exceptions, such as robberies or violent outbursts at work. One such situation I recall well involved three female employees of a prominent Ontario hospital, who got into a roll-about-the-floor fight in the outpatient area. A disturbing sight, I imagine, for the patients waiting there to meet with their consultant. This particular incident was racially motivated; one woman suggested to the other, and not too politely, that she return to her country of origin. Another incident involved an elderly lady who walked into the branch of a Canadian bank carrying a basket of Christmas goodies. She put the basket up on the counter and handed a note to the teller: *There's a bomb in the basket. Give me all your money!* But these two episodes are unusual (for a variety of reasons). Men perpetrate most violence.

Age

It has been our experience at the Trauma Response Service that men in their mid-thirties to mid-forties initiate most violence. In listening to the media, members of the public are often left with the impression that the violent offender in this country is the 18- to 25-year-old black male, but my experience does not reflect this. Most commonly, the violent individual is a more "mature" male who has let his rage build for a long time.

Race

"Waspy" is probably a reasonable word to describe the most common violent offender in the workplace: the white, Anglo-Saxon (but not necessarily Protestant) male. Contrary to popular opinion, the profile of the violent offender does not fit the young black man that we so often find portrayed in the media.

Projection

It is fairly common to find that people with an aggressive disposition are quick to blame others for things that go wrong for them. In other words, they can do no wrong themselves. In the work setting, the person who is the least aggressive is the one the violent person will blame for causing all the trouble.

"Rigid" Background

The person who has all the signs of being the problem in the workplace will often have a view of the world that might best be described as black-and-white, right-and-wrong or good-and-bad. Frequently, this comes from a fairly rigid religious upbringing, in which not a lot of interpretation is given to the "spirit" of the belief system, and more attention paid to the "letter" of, for example, the Bible or the Koran.

Recent Life Stressor

For many offenders, what precipitates an episode of rage is a difficult or stressful situation, either in their personal life or in their work life. The most recent example of this reported in the media was that of the broker from Atlanta, Georgia, who, after a large loss on the stock market, bludgeoned to death his wife and children, and then shot and killed a number of his colleagues. Not all episodes are so tragic, and not all hit the media, fortunately. An example that comes to mind for me—and that had a positive outcome—was that of an employee in a factory who was not performing his job very well in one area. His managers decided to move him to another post within the plant, thinking that he would do better there. Within days of the move, he began to make threatening statements to a colleague about the three managers involved. It started with his saying to the colleague, "I'm going to get those SOBs." The next day it was "I'm going to kill them." The next day it was "I've picked out a gun to get them." The next day it was "The gun arrives tomorrow!" The next day he said openly that he did not care who got in the way when he was shooting, as long as he managed to get the three bosses who were causing him pain! Only on the next day did the colleague report the matter to the organization, and then swift action was taken to deal with the situation. The police were informed, and the threatening individual was taken away for questioning. While the stressor in this case is obvious, it is not *always* so obvious. Often the employer does not know—and will never know—what is happening in the lives of employees outside working hours.

Addictive Personality

Potentially aggressive individuals often currently have—or have had in the past—a problem with alcohol, drug or other substance abuse. Most managers and supervisors are already aware of the signs of abuse at work, and look out for such signs as absences on Mondays and Fridays, a change in the individual's appearance, and long breaks taken during the workday. The typical person prone to work rage will more than likely be having difficulty controlling addictive behaviors. In one recent example, a man from a factory told his boss that he was dreaming about coming to work

bound with a belt of high explosives. He also said that
he was going to kill his girlfriend. This particular man
was known to have had an addiction to crack cocaine,
and the area in which he lived had a reputation as one of
the worst in the city for crack abuse. It was also discovered that his girlfriend was a user.

Paranoid Thinker

People are always talking about this person behind his
back, making comments about his appearance, his behavior, his lifestyle, anything—or so he believes. Many of
the more serious cases we hear about in the media seem
to pinpoint this part of the typical profile. Paranoia was
reported in the man who carried out the dreadful killings
that occurred at O.C. Transpo in Ottawa in 1999. It has
also been reported in the personalities of those involved
in the various tragic school shootings reported during
the past couple of years throughout North America. In
many of my recent consultations, these individuals have
had a high degree of paranoid thinking—without any
foundation in reality—about the way they are treated by
their organization.

Loner

Everyone wants to point a finger at the loner as the one
to beware of at work. This is partly due to the fact that
it's easy to spot the loner, and since we do not get to
know him very well, we assume that he is up to no good.
While it is true that the person who does not socialize

easily or make small talk or connect well with others can turn out to be a person full of rage, it is not always the case. Being a loner is, however, a significant part of the overall profile. The isolated person, the withdrawn person, the one who does not mix well or who is almost antisocial should be regarded with caution, especially if there are other particular attributes or warning signs in his work-related behavior.

History of Confrontational Behavior

This is, perhaps, one of the most important features of the profile. Anyone who is going to be a danger in the workforce will already be known to colleagues and friends as someone who can't control his temper and who seems to thrive on confrontation. Arguments develop easily, often out of thin air and without much provocation. The person is often known for his confrontational attitude toward peers and perceived authority. In my dealings with many organizations, I am often amazed at how little attention is paid to people who easily become aggressive. I have encountered situations in which the confrontational person has been allowed to blow up in a fit of rage at colleagues regularly for periods of up to 25 years or more, and yet nothing is done to address his behavior. Others write it off, saying, "That's just the way he is!" I find that frightening.

Unusual Interest in Weapons and the Military

It's often the case that the person also has either a collection of guns or an unusual interest in different types of weapons. This can sometimes be recognized in the magazines he reads or in the videos and movies he tells his colleagues about at work. Often if the person does not own a weapon himself then he will at least have access to a weapon of some description. In a fairly large number of prominent cases reported in recent years, the perpetrators of gross violence have been ex-military.

Diagnosed or Undiagnosed Mental/Emotional Illness

Many people who become aggressive and act out their rage at work are described as unstable, different, bizarre, or even plain weird. I can think of many examples of violence, well known to the general population and from my own experiences, involving people described in this way. They just do not fit our definition of "normal." Again, by way of illustration, in the days following the O.C. Transpo shootings in Ottawa, the media described Pierre LeBrun as "emotionally unstable," or even "depressed." But no account that I read was able to pinpoint just what it was about him that *made* him unstable. To use another illustration, some of the teenagers involved in the school shootings both in the U.S. and Canada have been described as behaving in a "depressed" way, or as "not quite themselves."

Certain mental illnesses can be at the root of rage behavior. For example, sufferers of paranoid schizophrenia, or any other psychotic illness, will often exhibit tendencies toward violent behavior. A friend of mine, usually one of the most laid-back and timid people in the world, once suffered a psychotic episode, and during a severe bout of the psychosis held a neighbor hostage, threatening to kill both himself and his hostage. The only thing that stopped that particular event from escalating was the quick intervention of police and paramedics.

Members of staff in psychiatric institutions are always at risk when treating illnesses such as schizophrenia and psychosis. In fact, health practitioners in the field of psychiatry are among those most at risk in North America for being on the receiving end of workplace violence.

Whether diagnosed or undiagnosed, mental illness of any kind, be it a fairly "simple" depression or a complex condition, should not be overlooked in trying to understand the background of a person likely to become violent. When we look with hindsight at the many major tragic events that have occurred in recent years, one of the factors that ties these together is the existence in the perpetrator of mental instability. Remember Dunblane, Scotland; Hungerford, England; Montreal, Quebec; Atlanta, Georgia; Taber, Alberta; Littleton, Colorado. Mental instability contributes greatly to the potential for rage. Employers cannot take chances with the safety of others by burying their heads in the sand, and saying, "That's just the way he is!"

For those in the workplace who have positions of responsibility for safety—and note that this includes almost everyone—the following list summarizes Early Warning Signs. When you identify an individual who seems to fit the profile, be aware that this person may need some supportive assistance from a professional. Take appropriate steps to document your observations, report what you see and discuss the situation with authoritative representatives within your own organization.

Early Warning Signs

- Changes in normal day-to-day behavior patterns—for example, lateness, increased sick time, hygiene, drop in quality of work or productivity
- Tendency to blame others for his own problems and weaknesses at work
- Rigid, black-and-white thinking
- Recent life stressor—for example, death, loss of job or relationship
- History of addictive behavior, alcohol, drug and substance abuse
- Tendency toward paranoid thinking, always worrying about what others are saying and thinking about him
- Isolation, inability to mix socially, lack of friends
- History of confrontational behavior, or increase in argumentativeness
- Unusual interest in weapons, the military
- Diagnosed or undiagnosed "instability" of a mental or emotional nature, described as "different" from normal or "strange"

Chapter 3

Rage—
The Who
and Where

There is a "dark side" to Gerry.

Now and again, I offer a colleague a ride home after work, or I drop him off at the gym. The ride from the office is always a short one, but during those moments we spend together in the vehicle, I let loose "the dark side." I hurl abuse at pedestrians. I make disparaging comments about the elderly. I scream at traffic lights. I ventilate with vigor on the craziness of Toronto traffic. Naturally, all of this is done with a sense of fun—the more I rant, the more I amuse my colleague, and the more fun I have. However, after a somewhat distressing day, after listening to the tales of tragedy and woe that is the norm in the world of Trauma Response, it does feel good to "have a go" at the world. And for the sake of the reader who may be wondering about my stability, let me reassure you that all of this "rage" activity happens with the vehicle windows tightly closed. My ranting is not directed at anyone in particular, nor is it done to cause offense. My behavior is very different from the behavior of one experiencing a surge of "road rage." Mine is a type of act; give me an audience, and I'll perform.

For many people, however, "rage" is *not* an act. It is a behavior over which they have little or no control, mainly because they have never learned how to identify the triggers, or starting points, for their rage; they have never "relearned" their errant behavior. With the best will in the world, a manager in an office or a plant floor, when faced with the rage of a disgruntled employee, will naturally respond to the rage with aggression, since that is probably the first and most spontaneous type of defensive response. Even if the manager is an in-tune person, whose communication skills are good, the likelihood is that she or he will try to rationalize the situation and ignore the emotion. Most people don't really want to deal with emotion, of any type, in the workplace.

The "who" and "where" of rage can sometimes be surprising, not to say awkward. During my time at university, I was involved in an incident of rage that shook the institution to its foundation. One of my classmates began to experience the unwanted and unsolicited attention of a female admirer in our class. Simonetta, a lovely young Italian woman, started to sit beside Robin, a blond, blue-eyed man from the American mid-west. Simonetta was in her late twenties; Robin was in his early twenties. All she did was sit beside him—every day. She did not speak to him; she just managed to sit beside him. And since Simonetta was always late for the start of class, it became a spectacle to see how she would manage to sit beside Robin. That was how it started.

After a while, she started to follow him outside the auditorium during breaks. All she did was walk behind him. No contact. No words. She just got into step a few paces behind him. (And, of course, all eyes in the class were observing ignominiously, and all tongues in the class started wagging ferociously. In a class of 200 students, that was quite a bit of ogling and wagging!) It got to the ridiculous point that she started following him into the men's washroom.

One day, after class had begun, the main door to the auditorium opened, and in walked Simonetta. The class professor had his back to the class and was writing on the chalkboard. A group of us had surrounded Robin on every side so as to prevent Simonetta from gaining access to him. Suddenly, she was climbing over the rows of seats and pushing people aside in order to get closer to Robin. She eventually managed to push someone out of the seat directly beside him. Robin had been watching her progress over the banked rows of seats, and you could see that his anger was growing. He became flushed and fidgety. No sooner had she sat on the chair next to him than he was on his feet, banging his fist on the desk in front of him. Suddenly he took a swing and hit her such a hard smack on the face that she fell, head over heels, landing flat on her back directly on top of the people seated there. Most of us just sat there in complete silence, incredulous that such a thing had happened. The professor, on turning round and observing the commotion, said, "This is a university. You can't behave like that here!" and returned to writing on the board.

I use this example to show how rage can make even the most unlikely people behave in uncharacteristic, and sometimes violent, ways. Robin was finally pushed too far. Incidentally, after the confrontation in class, Robin decided to continue his education back in the U.S. We later heard that members of Simonetta's family were aware that she had been suffering a mental illness for some time.

Although there may be some predictability in patterns, there are times when rage and violence are the things you least expect in your environment. None of us in class with Robin ever suspected that he would be enraged to the point of engaging in serious physical assault, but none of us could know exactly what Simonetta was putting him through. And I guess most of us were in some kind of denial about the possibility of danger for either of them. Being young and having had little exposure to rage at that point obviously contributed to our inaction. But it certainly made all of us in that class think carefully. And it made the university senate take action to protect students by introducing policies and security measures.

Rage happens at work. For our professor at university, the auditorium was his workplace, but even he could not do anything constructive to prevent the situation. Years later, it is easy for me to say now that we should not have ignored the signals. All of us must act to prevent violence from emerging at work, and that means we must be educated enough to know from which direction rage is likely to come, and from whom. There are various sources of violence and rage in the workplace, and I now want to share a few words on these sources.

Rage from Strangers

Of the more than 300 violent events to which Warren Shepell Consultants provides Trauma Response support each year, approximately 50 percent involve armed robbery. The usual targets of this type of robbery violence are banks and other financial institutions, department stores, convenience stores, gas bars and the like, by people who are *strangers* to the workplace. They come under the pretense of being customers, but their intention is not to make a purchase. Most of the time, these people have no legitimate relationship to the workplace, and their intentions are malicious. Currently in Canada, this group constitutes the largest group of perpetrators of workplace violence.

Rage from Customers

A growing group within Trauma Response is people at risk from irate customers. I get many calls every week regarding situations in which employees providing customer service are attacked, either verbally or, sometimes, physically, during the course of their duties as customer service agents. Whether it be at the counter of a tax office, at a service reception for spare parts, or waiting in line to see a physician in a health-care environment, many employees looking after the needs of customers suffer abuse. This type of rage becomes very personal, since the person at the counter, wherever that may be, is, for the customer, the "face" of the organization. All the frustrations of the customer become directed and aimed at the employee, who just happens to be the one servicing the customer counter at that moment. For whatever reason, many Canadians will automatically vent their rage in an aggressive and angry way at the first person they see, rather than looking constructively for solutions to their complaints.

Certainly, there are situations in life in which one might suppose that a client would become aggressive, such as when a police officer takes a criminal into custody, or a correctional officer deals with an inmate in a correctional facility, or a health-care worker in a psychiatric hospital copes with an individual whose particular mental illness tends toward aggression. For the most part, though, violent behavior that occurs in dealing with the customer or client is unexpected and situational.

Rage from a Co-Worker

When I talk about the rage of the co-worker, I try earnestly to keep my definitions broad, since the word *co-worker* can mean different things to different people. For example, people who leave or who are terminated from organizations can and do return to the workplace with malicious intent. A prime example of this occurred in 1999, when Pierre LeBrun, a resigned employee of O.C. Transpo in Ottawa, returned to the premises of his previous employer to fatally shoot four of his former colleagues and wound two others, before killing himself. Another occurred in Winnipeg in 1998, when a terminated employee from a large hospital forced his way into the human resources department and shot and killed the director. *Co-worker* can be defined as anything from current employee or manager to prospective employee, and must always include former employees or managers.

In today's society, where human rights are highly guarded, it can be extremely difficult to find out much information about prospective employees. Reference checking amounts to "Worker X was employed here between these dates. He had a satisfactory performance." And when we ask to speak "off the record" in an attempt to find out more, our efforts are in vain. We all know there is no such thing as "off the record." This makes it all the more difficult for employers to be proactive in creating a safe environment for staff. And when it comes to preventing former employees from doing harm later, that becomes even trickier. How can we predict if and when someone will take revenge on the organization? Of course, we can take steps to alert Security after an employee leaves of his or her own volition, or is terminated. But how can you stop the person with a malicious frame of mind from entering a school, a hospital, a college or a public place where security in minimal? It's not easy. It is not possible to predict violence; some is random. And it becomes a near-impossibility, therefore, to provide absolute security for employees in facilities where openness is a must.

Despite what I've said about the limitations of predicting, there are steps that employers can take to enhance workplace safety, and I will have more to say about this in another chapter. What's important here is the fact that rage can enter the workplace from any angle, from any hierarchical level, and can produce effects that traumatically impact on the immediate work environment as well as extend beyond the walls of the actual workplace.

Rage from Relations

Many incidents of workplace rage have been triggered by a member of an employee's immediate family. The family member—a spouse, significant other, child or parent, or some other person of a close relationship to the employee—shows up at the workplace to continue a confrontation resulting from a personal dispute. Many workplaces are affected by the rage ensuing from, for example, the break-up of a relationship, a bitter family quarrel or a disgruntled teenager. Situations of stalking are among the most acrimonious results of broken relationships.

Not long ago, I had to provide trauma support in such a case. A young woman who worked for a large telecommunications company decided to end the relationship with her boyfriend. Within a short period, he began to call her at work, leaving threatening messages about his imminent suicide. He also began to stalk her. No one really knows why she did not take steps to protect herself by reporting the stalking to the police. At the end of one working day, the ex appeared at the door of her workplace. As she tried to exit the building, he pulled a gun from his pocket and shot her dead on the doorstep. It was a tragic event, and one that was, perhaps, avoidable. Typically in these types of incidents, the perpetrator—in this case the ex-boyfriend—finds his way to the work environment to harass, threaten, injure or kill.

When a personal relation is involved in a workplace situation of aggression, it is not uncommon for colleagues to maintain a distance. No one wants to get involved. It is none of their business. When an aggressive wife or a screaming husband tries to continue a family dispute in our workplace, all we want to do is stay out of it. Of course, we are concerned about our colleague's well-being and safety, but not to the extent that we want to get involved. We turn a blind eye, as they say. And our negligence in doing so can lead to the unthinkable.

When I look back at the wide variety of rage situations in which I have been involved, either as a witness or as a *crisis responder*, I am amazed at how much I do not know about the subject, the effects, the "toxicology" of violence. At one time or another, I have encountered all of the various types of perpetrators I've described above. I have been touched, saddened and dismayed at my encounters with violent tragedy that could so easily have been avoided. I have learned much from all of these situations, and I continue to learn daily.

That said, I hope you, the reader, will not approach the workplace with a suspicious air regarding everyone and everything you see, expecting rage to rear its ugly head at any moment. That would be alarming. However, I do hope that I've conveyed to you the fact that given the right circumstances, rage can come from almost anyone.

The "where" of rage is a little easier to explain. The workplace is any location, permanent or temporary, where an employee performs a work-related duty. This has interesting consequences in the area of employer liability, as we will discuss in Chapter 11.

Increasingly in our society, the borders of the workplace are widening. There is a growing number of mobile employees; a growing number of "telecommuters," that is, people working from home by means of computers and the Internet; a growing number of employees "hoteling," booking into an office for a day and using shared space. This undoubtedly makes it all the more difficult for employers to provide for the safety and security of employees. For example, despite the security measures banks introduce—bulletproof glass, video surveillance, silent alarms, even on-site security guards—nothing will deter a robber. You can prepare for the unthinkable, hoping that the unthinkable will never happen, but you can't be *sure* that it will not happen. Some bank branches are known to be robbed regularly, month after month, even with the most up-to-date security systems. And in mentioning the banks, I do not imply that employees there are more or less vulnerable than anyone else. I use them only as an excellent example of how even an institution that takes proactive security measures cannot ensure the safety of its employees. The banks in Canada spend millions of dollars every year on protective measures—money well invested, I would say—but it still does not stop them from being robbed about 1,300 times a year! Even the most secure workplace will be vulnerable to violence. Still, that should not deter employers from taking every possible step to provide for the safety and security of employees in their work locations, wherever those locations may be.

Just as an organization such as Canada Post can take steps to protect the mail deliverer from the sharp teeth of the aggressive dog (by making alternative arrangements for that household), so can all employers take steps appropriate to their particular business. Measures for the provision of safety can be fairly simple. It really depends on the circumstances. The following, not listed in priority, are examples of some protective measures:

Protective Measures

- Securing entry to and exit from a building.
- Issuing identity cards, especially in larger organizations. Unknown persons or strangers to the organization can then be spotted more easily.
- Putting policies in place for staff required to carry out home visits, and defined action plans for them to get out when there is any kind of danger.
- Making use of user-friendly security systems as a deterrent to robbery.
- Installing good lighting in the staff car parking area.
- Providing traveling employees with a company-paid cell phone. Aid is then only a quick call away.
- Having good communications around potentially dangerous family members and relatives approaching the workplace.
- Making good use of restraining orders or bonds when the need arises.
- Using good architecture in the functional design of customer service counters, with an eye to employee safety.
- Positioning cash counters a good distance from the door, especially in banks, retail outlets and smaller stores.

Chapter 4

The Rage
of the Bully

As a young and, I sometimes think, fairly naïve priest, I was introduced to the rage of the bully. At the time, I often questioned the attitudes and behavior of my fellow priests. For people who were considered to be role models of Christianity, they were involved in antics on a daily basis that not only surprised but upset me. Some of these "men of God" were so far removed from God that they treated their fellow human beings with contempt, and even disgust. That's not to say that there were not some among them who were, indeed, the holy men one expected to find in the priesthood, but, unfortunately, I had to look hard to find them.

The bully in question was what is known in Scotland as the parish priest, and I had been assigned to be his assistant. At the time of my appointment, I was not very happy about being sent to work with him, since he already had an established reputation for "breaking" people. At least two others who had previously worked with him had left his company as saddened and emotionally bereft people. However, since I really had no choice in the matter, I took up residence in his household with a fairly positive attitude—as positive as it could be for someone who was not really happy with his lot in life as a priest, anyway! It quickly became apparent to me, and to a colleague, another assistant in the same household, that the reputation this man had was well earned. Only the close connection to and solidarity with my colleague made life tolerable during the three years I spent in that assignment.

This person demonstrated the characteristics of a bully in many ways. For example, it became clear to me within a short time that he was spreading malicious and unfounded rumors about me. He would engage me in public humiliation, openly criticizing my work. Often, he would go into a rage over very trivial matters. His criticism of others, too, was persistent. Listening to another's point of view was never on his agenda. His sense of control over everything was absolute, even to deciding what we would eat and drink. He could be vindictive, hostile and devious, and at the same time charming to outsiders or to his superior. He was always right; everyone else was useless.

At the time, I don't suppose I regarded the situation with any objectivity, since I was right in the middle. It's only with years of hindsight that I can now say this with certainty: the priest was a bully. And his rage was something to be feared. Although I never for one moment worried that he would turn his shotgun on me—he was

also a hunter and owned a collection of hunting rifles!—
there were times when he made me feel as though I might
use one of those guns on him! (Thankfully, thinking
about something and seeing the thought through to
fruition are two different things.) After a long period of
three years, and approaching nervous exhaustion, I
requested and was granted a new assignment in another
town about 30 miles away.

Years have now passed and thousands of miles of
distance separate me from the events of that time, but one
important message stems from the telling of this story.
The rage of a bully creates a poisoned atmosphere in any
workplace. The domineering, controlling style of
management that is used to demean people through
cruelty is one of the major causes of workplace violence.
There are other causes, of course, and these will be elabo-
rated upon later, but for now I want to share a few
thoughts on the rage of the bully in the Canadian context.

Among Canadian workers, I consider myself to be
highly privileged. I am allowed to see the "heart and
soul" of organizations, especially during the period after
a tragedy or a downsizing when I work closely with
representatives of the entire organization, from executive
officers to the rank-and-file. People tell me things they
would never tell anyone else: the deep, dark secrets that
never make the headlines. I am entrusted with delicate
and sensitive information, and I value the trust placed in
me very highly.

I am often amused and frequently disappointed,

however, by what I hear, especially the great divergence of opinion within organizations about their own management "style." From the senior executives, I hear about all the wonderful management techniques and styles they endorse and encourage, and which they introduce into their environment at a cost of tens of thousands of dollars. Most commonly, I learn about the values of team-building, coaching, mentoring and collaborative management styles. From the same source, I hear of the great efforts taken to empower employees in decision-making, and I am constantly told, "We encourage our staff to creatively share their opinions." When I ask the same executives if they have any "bullies" in the management team, I am reminded politely that the controlling methods of the past are no longer seen in today's workplace. *Bravo!*

And then I get to listen to the staff in these same organizations. Do we get convergence of opinion? Certainly not. I work with many organizations—small, medium and huge—and I find the results of my nosy interest at the grass-roots level different from the results at the executive level.

I often tell senior members of an organization that if they want to know how effective communication is within their organization, they should just ask the people at the bottom of the hierarchical ladder. If these employees are able to accurately present messages that have come from the top, then the communication process is probably good. The same thing applies to management style. If an organization really wants to know what style of management is perceived to be encouraged within the company, all they have to do is ask the people on the receiving end. It's such an easy process, and, at the same time, perhaps too simple. Management would often rather hire another consultant to tell them!

The reality is this: in many of the organizations throughout Canada where I have had the opportunity to ask groups of employees simple questions about management style within their company, the results are surprisingly similar—and very alarming. I realize that in putting this to paper, many organizations will feel offended and even slighted, since I present no empirical data to support my case, but my experience indicates that a controlling, domineering style of management is still prevalent in Canada.

When I ask groups of employees about their managers, I get similar responses across the entire country:

- They control us.
- They ask our opinion and then they tell us the way it's going to be.
- They do not show us any respect.
- The only time we see them is when we have done something wrong.
- They treat us as numbers.
- They don't even know my name.

On the other side of the fence, managers make such comments as the following:

- You're lucky even to have a job!
- Don't ask—just do it.
- I have the power, I can fire you any time!
- You're not paid to think.

Occasionally, I encounter an organization that really does practice what it preaches, or "walks the talk." But I can say with great certainty that the companies that really do a lot of talking and walking are few and far between. There is a lot of talking but very little walking out there in the big wide world of management.

The potential for rage in these controlling organizations is going to be higher, and for several reasons. When you have a mentoring, coaching and collaborative management style, employees tend more toward higher productivity, efficiency and effectiveness, and there is a happier workplace atmosphere. Conversely, when there is a domineering, controlling or even bullying environment, the employees feel threatened, are less productive, feel highly stressed and are unhappy. The theory of the short leash does not apply to us humans: when people are highly stressed and feel intimidated, their potential for aggression grows, and so does the potential for violence in the workplace.

It's always fascinating to me to find out as much as possible about the leader in any organization, whomever it may be—a president, a chief executive officer or a managing director. Much of the "corporate culture" takes its lead from the top. For example, if the person at the top is perceived to be a controlling person, you'll probably find many of the middle managers will emulate the controlling style. When the leader is a mentor and a guide, many of the "followers" will also be guides. And it does not really matter what is written in the company Vision or Mission Statement or Guiding Principles—or whatever form the company's formal philosophy takes. Very few organizations really adhere to their own written statements.

Most of the guiding principles of organizations tend to be found in the "subconscious" culture, where cultural norms have been passed on from generation to generation and are relived in the day-to-day life of the company. And keep in mind that a "generation" in an organization may only be the time since the last restructuring or downsizing! Most of the time the standard is set at the top, so if you want to know how people are really treated by their employer, look at how the top people treat their own direct reports.

When the person at the helm of an organization is known as, and is seen to be, a "control freak," there is perceived to be tacit permission that "controlling" is an acceptable form of behavior within the company. On the other hand, when there is genuine listening, authentic collaboration and visible, motivational leadership from the top, the organization is seen and felt to be accepting of creativity from its staff. You find in the latter case a better, more empowering atmosphere all round.

Of course, some readers will make quick judgments about my observations, and will think of many valid reasons why there needs to be a certain level of control within an organization. But the type of control that I am describing here does not include the practical measures that organizations have to use in order to remain competitive, such as quality controls and standards. I am talking about the *management method* with which action is taken, the type of abuse of power that makes staff in organizations feel threatened, intimidated, useless and devalued as persons. No one can convince me that this type of "control management" is not alive and thriving in Canada.

It is a must that employees of every creed, color, race, religion, size, shape, ability and disability be treated with respect in their chosen work environment. It matters not whether we as individuals consider the job to be a menial task or the most important position in the world. Position, status, place, earnings, location, responsibility—these are all relative. All of us as employed human beings are guaranteed dignity and respect through our federal or provincial human rights codes. Yet one of the major areas of discontent in the Canadian workplace arises from the fact that employees do not feel respected, and this is particularly the case when there is a controlling boss running the operation. It is my opinion that one of the biggest contributors to the problem of rage in the workplace is the growing lack of respect for people as people that is endemic to Canada. Any organization, therefore, that wants to stand out as a "good company to work for" has to be extremely vigilant in how it *selects, trains and promotes* into management. Management sets the tone for the entire organization.

Selecting Managers

Recognizing how difficult it can be to conduct reference checks these days, it therefore becomes mandatory for organizations to ensure that their recruitment policies and procedures are as comprehensive as possible. If an organization really wants to attract a certain type of employee with real "people skills"—often referred to as the "soft skills"—it has to make sure there are methods in place to test for and even demonstrate this set of skills. This can be done through role-playing in the interview process, through psychological assessment and psychometric testing, and by having specialists in the art of human resources recruitment available to the organization, either full-time, in-house professionals or consultants. It is often worth spending a few more dollars up front in the recruitment process, rather than having to pay later in terms of employee discontent. For example, when considering how many dollars are to be spent to advertise available positions, consider, too, how many dollars will be set aside for the actual recruitment process in terms of interviewing, testing and using the professional expertise now widely available. Investing wisely pays dividends.

Training Managers

The process of learning to be a manager is just beginning on the day of selection. When an organization wants to be certain that the philosophical principles of respect and dignity for all are being demonstrated, the organization leaders must take on the responsibility of measuring the performance of managers. The organization has to ensure that managers are trained to turn the philosophy of respect into a reality. So with the understanding that respect involves tolerance, acceptance of others, patience, caring, willingness and a host of other attributes, it becomes indispensable for managers to have the skill-set necessary to model these attributes. Ongoing training is a must in the following nine areas:

1. Assertiveness in communication
2. Understanding the influence of alcohol, drug and other substance abuse in the workplace
3. Effective management of disability in the workplace
4. Cross-cultural sensitivity
5. Conflict resolution and negotiation
6. Dealing with aggression
7. Stress management
8. Visible management in busy times
9. Motivational management

Promoting Managers

Over the years, I have heard some of the strangest reasons why people are promoted into management.

Here are some examples:

- She gets things done!
- He's been around a long time—now it is his turn.
- She deserves it.
- We've no other place to move him except up.
- Let's see how badly she does this.
- Maybe he can do better than the last one.
- She's got a real reputation for being tough. She'll straighten them all out.
- He's a hatchet man—he'll get our numbers down.

Such comments come mostly from disgruntled members of staff. Recently, I had the experience of working with an organization on what is known as a *change management* issue. Staff in a particular department were experiencing difficult times after a downsizing. While doing the normal initial assessment with my organizational contact, I asked if there had been other changes that might be affecting the group's ability to recover. My contact person, a human resources professional, then advised me that a new director had been appointed. When I asked her what this man was like and how the staff perceived him as a manager, I was told that of the likely candidates for this post, he was the last person the staff would have chosen. They detested him as a colleague, never saw eye to eye with him, and did not respect his work ethic. And now management had promoted him! (Sometimes I really am set up for failure.)

The message received by the staff from the organization was very negative. When I eventually started working with them, they told me their greatest concern was that this particular person did not respect anyone in the workplace. They felt threatened by his appointment to management. Prior to his appointment, they had enjoyed a harmonious relationship with their director, a person who visibly practiced respectful management.

When organizations are in the process of promoting staff to management, they should be careful to make sure that whoever is being promoted has not only the skill-set required to fulfill the job function, but also the "soft skill-set" that will ensure the establishment of harmonious, respectful relationships among staff.

My unfortunate experience as a young priest, tormented internally because of my unsettled attitude to the priesthood, and tormented externally by a bully, obviously affected my thinking, my judgment and my general outlook on life at that time. It does take effort and time to recover from the draining effects of that kind of controlling management. I am extremely lucky that I bounced back, made some life decisions for the better in the following year, and recovered well. However, in the course of years of working in employee assistance, I have encountered many individuals whose confidence and self-esteem is almost nonexistent, entirely due to the long-lasting effects of the rage of the bully. How sad. And how sad does it have to get before the sadness is redirected as rage?

Chapter 5

Rage in the Work System

When I begin to identify a problem with rage in a particular organization, I find it easy to become judgmental, point a finger. It's easy to say, "Yes, of course, you have a bully manager and he must be at fault." It's easy to blame ineffective reference checking, or a host of other factors, for an employee bringing a gun to work with the intention of shooting his manager.

In reality, it is difficult to pin down exactly why some organizations are prone to violent outbursts from staff while others sail along softly in the wind without any trouble. It is true that some organizations tend to see more aggression than others. But statistically speaking, it is hard to identify a trend, for reasons alluded to earlier in this work—that is, an absence of reliable statistical data on rage in the workplace in Canada.

That said, certain factors have been identified as contributing to some companies experiencing higher levels of violence than others. These are known as *system characteristics*, indicating where violence is more prevalent. As already stated, I do not really intend to do an in-depth study of the reasons for workplace violence. Rather, recognizing that rage does exist, I intend to probe some of the roots of violence, looking at where rage exists and postulating what we can do about it. There are obvious influences outside the workplace that contribute to the increasing frequency of episodic rage at work. Yet, paradoxically, North American homicide rates are going down, while workplace assaults are on the rise.

The Influence of the Media

Among the influences outside the workplace, who can deny the power of the media, where the portrayal of violence is almost constant, and at times, intoxicating? The more we get, the more we seem to want. We witness thousands upon thousands of gratuitous homicides every year on TV; we see beatings and stabbings, shootings and rapes, sometimes all within a 20-minute segment. We argue that it's only dramatization and that it's not real, so it can't possibly affect us. Or does it? There are studies indicating that seeing violence on television leads to the perpetration of violence, as well as studies indicating that to even think this is crazy. So directors and producers continue to create more tempting, tasteless and usually tragic shows to entertain us into the wee hours. Whatever the truth may be, one thing is certain: violence attracts the viewing public. We only have to watch any television news program to recognize that the stories getting the top billing, the prime space, are usually about the after-effects of rage. It is indeed interesting that something we abhor is also something that so fascinates us.

The Influence of Drug Proliferation

Another factor influencing the workplace in Canada is the widespread availability of illegal drugs. Take a walk down some of the main streets in Canada's largest cities, and in no time at all the evidence of drug infestation becomes very clear. It is logical to deduce that if availability of drugs is widespread on the street, then there will also be ample supply in the workplace. When there is systemic abuse of drugs in society, the workplace is not exempt.

The trouble with some drugs is not just the addictive nature, but the harmful side-effects that they induce in personality and thought patterns. In habitual users, a raised level of aggressive behavior is not unusual. Addiction leads not only to aggression, but to higher incidence of violent robbery, if the addicted person has to find illegal ways to pay for a fix.

The Influence of Politics and Economics

I am not really a political animal. Like most Canadians, I probably have a healthy disrespect for politics and care more about tax cuts than about who becomes the next mayor of Toronto. That's not to say that I do not have an awareness of the problems associated with cuts in social programs that hit the marginalized members of our society more than they do the middle classes. When there are high levels of poverty, high unemployment, greater demands on food banks and a large number of welfare recipients, the aggression levels in society rise. Of course, we hear on a regular basis that the number of welfare recipients drops month by month in Ontario, but it would seem that the rules for eligibility are like constantly changing goal posts, and do not really reflect the actual number of people needing social assistance. Homelessness continues to grow at an alarming rate and some of the food banks cannot cope with demand. These kinds of pressures within society can be reflected in the workplace, especially in the way that today's employers, particularly in the service industries, tend to hire people on a contract basis—without benefits, and often at minimum wage.

I don't intend to stand on any political platform, but just to raise an issue that I think exists. There are many disappointed, angry people in our society for whom there seems to be no hope. Sadly, many are affected by racism, sexism, ageism, bigotry, discrimination, systemic oppression and poverty. It is ironic, as noted earlier, that the United Nations still points to Canada as one of the best places in the world to live. The nature of the country's political and economic life must somehow be reflected in the workplace. And I personally believe that there are external factors contributing to Canada's high levels of workplace violence, when compared to other countries in the world.

The Influence of Restructuring and Downsizing

Ask anyone in the workplace what they crave most, next to their paycheck, and you will discover an entire world in search of stability and security. They're out of luck. Twenty or thirty years ago, it was part of the psychological makeup of the work contract: you could almost be guaranteed security of tenure in many occupations. With the changes in organizational philosophy over the past 10 years, however, job security is a thing of the past.

In my work as a change management consultant, another hat I wear for my current employer, I encourage people attending my workshops to think more about commitment to the job at hand than loyalty to the organization. I ask them to prepare to be a marketable commodity rather than a faithful employee. I propose that they maintain expectations of themselves rather than develop an "entitlement" mentality. An entitlement mentality I understand as an attitude of mind which says, "I am loyal to my employer, therefore I am entitled to good benefits, a good pension, good compensation and long-term security in the job." Often I encourage people to take ownership and responsibility for their own career path, rather than settle for a secure job. No matter what I teach or encourage, however, people still crave that security in their employment.

Over the past five years, I have acted as a consultant, workshop facilitator and counselor to many organizations going through the process of restructuring and downsizing. It has been often interesting, sometimes exciting and frequently frustrating. I am convinced that one of the main reasons for the high levels of stress in the workplace, and for the resulting high levels of aggression and rage, is the constant fast pace of workplace change. Staff affected by restructuring, re-engineering, work-force adjustment or rightsizing, end up having to do more with less—more work with fewer resources. They have to learn new technology if they want to stay ahead. The demands from the employer in terms of time commitment to the job are in many cases extreme. People are just expected to do what is required without a word of complaint; their negativity will not be seen as a career-enhancing move!

With many organizations, I have encountered a true spirit of regret by leaders when a major upheaval that leads to layoffs is announced. Good planning, good severance packages, the human touch in the termination process—all these contribute to a smooth downsizing with as little pain and trauma as possible. In some of these organizations, I have watched managers and human resources professionals make agonizing decisions, but in the most humane and professional way possible. But when the opposite occurs, when an organization acts callously and demonstrates little respect for terminees and survivors, then the danger of aggression is greatly enhanced.

I remember dealing with a community college during a period of cutbacks under that particular provincial education budget. The college administration sent around a secretary to deliver the layoff notices, which were left on the professors' desks without so much as a word. Needless to say, I do not think this is an appropriate way to deliver the bad news.

There is no *good* method for downsizing, but there are some techniques that make the process less painful. Public "herding" of employees into groups of terminees and survivors is also on my list of not-so-good ways. Whereas, I would rank holding private, individual meetings, no matter how long they take to accomplish, as one of the more humane and professional ways of delivering the bad news. Other small details that make the process more caring and less painful include providing outplacement consulting or psychological counseling as part of the exit process. It makes a big difference to those who remain within the organization if the terminees have been seen to be treated with dignity and respect. It helps to provide some kind of trauma counseling for the survivors of downsizing, so they can begin the grieving process that is so essential, especially when the organization wants to kick-start "moving forward." It's like driving a car, really. If you want to "move forward" safely, you must "look back" over your shoulder to make sure that the road is clear and that it is now safe to step on the gas and get into the traffic. Similarly, in any post-restructuring organization, in order to move forward, employees need to be provided the opportunity to ventilate bad feelings about—look back at—the loss of friends, colleagues, good relationships and organizational culture resulting from the restructuring.

When restructuring is handled badly, it is likely that there will be overt expression of aggression from terminees, survivors and even members of the local community.

The Influence of Strikes

What is it about a labor dispute that brings out the worst aggression in people? During my life, I have seen many examples of the absolute horror that arises when there is a strike. I remember the miners' strike in the United Kingdom in the 1970s, and the violence that erupted in the mass riots all over the country at that time. More recently, I witnessed the Ontario government employees' strike that caused a lot of bitterness and pain throughout the province. And what about the memorable teachers' strike, during which we heard of death threats, obscene calls and even attacks on the property of school board members, principals and vice principals. There were personal attacks on many at the picket line, and not only by teachers but also by irate parents who wanted the teachers back at work! How is it that this type of rage, which causes damage that takes years to repair, even erupts?

An opportunity came my way a number of months ago to be a member of a *post-strike response team*. I was invited to work with a team that included two human resources professionals, one of whom was a bit of an international troubleshooter in labor relations; the other was a consultant in alternative dispute resolution who was a former executive of a large union. I would fill out the team as the trauma response specialist. We all flew in to our location ready to investigate what had gone wrong for this organization and what could now be done to remedy the situation at the start of the new contract. Our briefing had been comprehensive, and we were very aware that the road to resolution had been long and bitter.

Being almost of one mind, we agreed immediately to speak with as many people at the organization as was humanly possible. Thus we began the process of working in focus groups, asking for frankness and honesty, and guaranteeing confidentiality to the participants. We interviewed a couple of hundred staff members over the next week or so, and managed to do some outreach to local dignitaries, RCMP and the local community. There were some unusual and highly political circumstances surrounding this particular dispute, and it was in the national and international interest that it end swiftly.

All the things you might expect to happen during a strike happened in this community: intimidation, harassment, physical and verbal threats, best friends becoming worst enemies at the picket line, family feuds developing over the conflicting status of management (a parent) crossing the picket line and staff (a family member) picketing. There were clashes between those exempt from striking and those who were obliged to strike, even though they personally did not want to be on strike. It had become acrimonious and dangerous. Fortunately, good sense prevailed due to astute local leadership of the union, and a new contract was eventually agreed upon after weeks of bickering and hardship.

Our task as a team was really to promote the healing process, much needed after the employees' return to work. People who had been friends were enemies. People who once were respected were finding themselves the objects of derision. Many could not find the energy just to say, "It's over, let's move on together!" It had indeed been a mess.

Our findings from the focus groups were fairly constant throughout the organization: staff members were unanimous about why things had become so bad that they felt strongly the need to strike. First on the list was the fact that the CEO was an unknown entity and was thought to be a "controller" rather than a "collaborator" in terms of management style. Most of the rank-and-file within the group of a couple of hundred staff had no experience of visible leadership—and not just from the CEO. Some of them did not even know who their immediate manager was!

A close second was the absence of good channels of communication. Many members of staff were often "out of the loop" when it came to what was happening in the organization. This lack of good, open, honest and factual information often contributes to rising stress levels within organizations.

Third, there was a perceived lack of respect by management toward the employees. The organization in other parts of the world prides itself on the way it demonstrates a caring, respectful attitude toward all staff, but this was the one thing everyone agreed was lacking at this site.

Fourth, there had been no real attempt to create a working management/labor relations committee. Everything became an issue with no resolution. The methods of dealing with issues then became adversarial, rather than collaborative. Added to the above four issues were others, such as massive downsizing in a small community, loss of rights and privileges, reductions in pay rates, changes in conditions of service. And there you have it—all the ingredients required to create a hostile environment. In some ways, it is not surprising that people became aggressive. Push people too far in one direction and they will push back!

It is not difficult to understand, therefore, that when conditions are tough and there has been "pushing" of employees by the employer for a long period of time, the risk of an aggressive strike becomes higher. In retrospect, when you look at the teachers' strike or the Ontario Public Service Employees Union dispute, one can conclude that the conditions had been ripe for a long time for an acrimonious strike.

Just what it is that makes the normally quiet individual succumb to mob rule, I am not sure. For two people to be friends one day, and suddenly, because of a strike, for the same two friends to be regarding each other aggressively, with rage, using words like "scab" and "scum," seems to me to be almost incomprehensible. Strikes can leave scars with people for years.

The Influence of Delegation Down the Ranks

As we investigate some of the influencing factors for organizational aggression or rage, I can't help wondering about organizations in which the senior executives absent themselves from any active responsibility for making the workplace safe. The "Do whatever you want, but don't bother us with the details" attitude actually prevails in some organizations. In the aftermath of the O.C. Transpo massacre, I have been consulted by many organizations regarding rage in the workplace and the potential for similar incidents in the future. My advice to all of them is that there is only a minuscule percentage of a chance that someone within their organization could do something similar, but that it is not worth gambling that it won't happen. Better safe than sorry.

For some strange reason, those at the top often do not want to step out on a limb and take responsibility for making the organization as safe from rage and aggression as it can be. Yes, they will agree to spend a few dollars on training a few people, or send a few delegates to a conference, but when it comes to an all-out attack on the problems associated with aggression at work, they seem to be in some state of denial. There may be well-founded reasons for this denial or neglect of duty, but I postulate that if a work environment is going to be made free from rage, we need the input and role-modeling of the most senior persons in the organization.

The Influence of Hiding Signals

There is a code of silence operating in some organizations, under which individuals in management do not share much information with each other about potential trouble spots. They observe aggressive behavior, sometimes deal with it, sometimes not, and then they keep the information to themselves, making no notes or recordings about it. It may not necessarily be deliberate collusion on their part to hide the behavior; it may be simple complacency. From a liability point of view, it may not be a good idea to keep that kind of information hidden, but from a purely human and safety point of view, it is actually dangerous. Turning a blind eye to aggression and ignoring the aggressor is like giving permission for all staff to behave similarly. It conveys clearly that misconduct is allowed in this organization. It hails the start of a poisoned environment and is one other factor that contributes to the systemic characteristics of a workplace where rage bubbles openly to the surface.

The external and internal influences that raise the profile of rage in the work "system" are probably many more than those outlined and described here. I have chosen the above-listed because I believe they indicate some of the main roots of violent behavior in the workplace today. Tremendous inroads can be made when we can identify *roots* that pave the way to describing *routes* to be followed to a problem's solution.

Chapter 6

Rage
from Home

Within a few weeks of my introduction to the world of
employee assistance, I was plunged into one of the worst
scenarios that, even to this day, I can imagine. When
most of us think about domestic abuse, we conjure up
the picture of a vicious spouse-beater who batters and
bruises his partner. The scene I attended to had no
resemblance to anything I had ever encountered, and
certainly was far removed from the spousal abuse that we
hear so much of today. The following is not a pretty
story, so *caveat lector*—"Let the reader beware!"

My colleague received a call from a department
supervisor who expressed concern over one of his staff.
The man in question—let's call him Ernie—was staying
in his workplace for long periods of time, sometimes
even sleeping there overnight. Ernie's behavior patterns
had changed subtly over the past few months. His
supervisor had noticed Eddie's appearance had become
sloppy, he was not relating to the supervisor well, and

he seemed to be withdrawn and at times highly agitated. Ernie worked in a public washroom as an attendant— not the ideal place in which to spend a lot of time, and certainly not one equipped for overnight visitors! He was in his mid-forties, described by his supervisor as a reasonable employee, but by the supervisor and colleagues as "rather strange." Given the type of work involved, it was not unusual to find out that people thought him strange. We had a number of people in this type of employment who would have found it fairly difficult to hold down any other job for any length of time.

Anyway, when the supervisor actually caught Ernie in the washroom after work, getting ready to bed down for the night, he asked him why he was not going to his own home to sleep. Ernie replied that he liked to walk to work, but that since he lived a good distance away, about 10 miles, he thought it would be easier to stay overnight so that he wouldn't be late to start the early shift the next day. The supervisor let Ernie know that the washroom was not to be used as a personal resting place after working hours. He was not to do it again.

Of course, he did it again. The supervisor caught him again, and asked if Ernie had understood their previous conversation. Ernie replied that he had, but that he was finding it too exhausting to walk as well as to work. The supervisor was just about to recommend that he make use of the public transit system, when Ernie said, "You're damn lucky I get here at all. I have to care for my elderly mother, and before I even get out of the house I have to tie her up in a chair."

Needless to say, that's when the call came to my colleague. What could we do about it? Our first reaction was fairly standard, and was probably based on our preconceived ideas about the type of people who worked in public washrooms. Our experience was that many of them were not well educated, came from humble social backgrounds and usually were employed there because of some physical or mental disability. It was a very judgmental approach—not very ethical for therapists! So when we discussed the situation with the supervisor, we really thought it was just a story, but we offered to investigate further.

Having decided to go and speak to Ernie, we drove to the location of the washroom and sought him out. We introduced ourselves and our function, then asked Ernie if we could speak to him regarding something he had said to his supervisor. Ernie said, "No, you can't. You're nothing but a couple of interfering busybodies! Just go away and leave me alone."

Not to be defeated so quickly, I challenged him on the grounds that he had said something to his colleague that indicated someone could be in danger, and we just wanted to help. However, nothing would shift him. He became very defensive, so much so that he would not even lift up his head to look directly in our eyes. He looked very disheveled, unshaven, untidy in appearance, and was beginning to get angry. Both my colleague and I began to experience that feeling in the pit of the stomach that says, "There's something seriously wrong here." I asked him directly about his mother, and he said that she was at home and she was well. Could we go to visit her? we asked. His reply was not inviting: "Just leave me alone and let me get on with my work. Have you nothing better to do than annoy me?" We returned to the car and looked at each other—it was a decisive moment. We were afraid that he had done something awful to his mother.

Our next stop was the police station closest to Ernie's home, just to inform them that we might be in need of their assistance later. Our intention was to visit Ernie's home to check that all was indeed well with his mother. We had already taken the preliminary step of asking the supervisor for Ernie's address and telephone number. Since there was no response to our telephone calls, we decided to head straight for his home, located in a very upscale suburb of Glasgow. On arriving, we found ourselves outside a home that certainly did not match our biased thinking about him: the place was palatial—a grand building, modern stucco and very large.

From the outside it looked deserted. All the drapes and blinds were drawn, windows were closed. There was no response to our ringing the doorbell.

We decided to try to get into the backyard, to see if there was any life at the other end of the house. Again, all the blinds were closed tight and no windows were open. I even climbed up one of the drainage pipes to get a look into the kitchen, which was high above the ground. But again, I couldn't see anything through the blinds.

On the spur of the moment, I decided to look in the house through the letterbox on the front door, and perhaps call out to Nell. As soon as I opened the box, I was hit on the face with the most powerful stench of human waste, urine, feces. It caught me so by surprise that I had to fight hard not to vomit. Even as I write about this dreadful experience, my skin crawls.

Well, the next step was to call the police. Something was obviously very wrong in that house. It took the police some time to arrive, since they wanted to pick up Ernie on the way, and let him explain, if there was anything to explain. Ernie arrived with two large police officers, one on either side. He fumbled in his pocket for his key, reached down to his feet, loosened his shoelaces, stopped to take off and pick up his shoes, and then opened the front door. I remember thinking at the time, "What a strange thing to do!" We asked him to show us to his mother, and he said that she was in the kitchen.

All of us entered the home cautiously, swooning and gasping for air, overwhelmed by the ferocious smell of human waste and rotting foodstuffs. Every inch of space on the floor was covered with garbage: stacks of magazines, half-full bottles of milk well on its way to cheese, packets of rotting cookies, rotting vegetables. It was a complete mess, but the overpowering smell of urine and feces was the worst I have ever encountered.

Having negotiated our way through the mess, we

eventually came to the door of the kitchen. One police officer entered first, followed by my colleague and then me. He immediately uttered a most heartfelt obscenity, and I could see why. There, lying on the floor in a puddle of indescribable filth, tied with rough parcel string to a small Formica kitchen chair, was the body of a very small, frail, elderly lady. She was breathing, and therefore alive, but she had the most horrible open, bleeding and suppurating wounds on both her legs and arms. Her face was so badly bruised that you could hardly see her eyes, and her torso was just a mass of bleeding and bruising. The wounds looked so bad that I thought they must be gangrenous. All of us were ready to pass out, but the sight of her helpless frailty made us keep control and fight the instinct to throw up.

Nell gained consciousness while we were waiting for the ambulance. She talked about her wonderful son, Ernie, and how she had become a handful for him. It was not his fault! she said. We asked her the last time she remembered being out of the house, and we were able to deduce that she had been tied to the chair and lying on the floor for more than four months.

What a horror story. She was a lovely wee lady, very articulate and nice to listen to. While waiting for the ambulance, she told stories of her past fortunes and misfortunes, and did not complain at all about the way we had found her—bleeding, in pain and neglected almost to the point of death. Nell was rushed off to the local emergency room, and admitted as a patient. Her injuries were so severe that the physicians thought she might not walk again and that she would have difficulty using her arms.

Ernie, too, was rushed off, but not to emergency. He was remanded for questioning at police headquarters. Later, he was released without charge. His treatment of his mother in this violent and despicable manner was deemed to be unintentional—the result of undiagnosed severe psychiatric illness. However, he was required to undergo ongoing counseling through employee assistance.

When I got home that night, it was getting late. I was tired, shocked, physically depleted and hungry because I hadn't eaten. I had previously arranged to have dinner with a friend and decided to keep the appointment. On arriving at my friend's apartment, I excused myself and went to the washroom, jumped fully clothed into the tub, removed my clothing, turned on the water and stayed there for at least 30 minutes, until I felt the smell had been purged.

Ernie was a very wealthy man. He played the stock market and, in fact, did not even need to work. But he was also a bit of a collector, particularly of magazines and newspapers relating to finances and investment. The day after Nell was admitted to hospital, we organized for the city's garbage collectors to visit the family home and start the cleanup of all the hazardous waste there. I was told that even the garbage collectors could not believe the amount of filth and waste. They filled more than 200 large black garbage sacks with the junk. I, for one, certainly did not envy their job.

Nell was eventually transferred to a retirement home and regained the use of her legs, but she was already in her eighties, and so the recovery was limited. Her mind, though, remained intact. My colleague and I visited her on a number of occasions and found her to be charming, witty and bright. Ernie was restricted in his visiting at first, mainly due to his lack of ability to comprehend the danger and the violence he had caused to his old mother. He came into counseling at our center, and eventually decided that seeking retirement on the grounds of his ill-health was his best option. Taking this decision also enabled him to have a considerable lump sum of money with which to pursue his avid interest in investments.

There is a moral to this story. Domestic violence has a habit of making itself known in the workplace, sometimes in the person of the victim, as in the case of a battered spouse, and sometimes in the person of the perpetrator, as in Ernie's case. The bizarre and unusual behavior that he was exhibiting affected his job performance, his attitude and even his appearance. The fact that the supervisor was able to note the differences in his behavior was much to his credit, and in the long term, his swift action probably saved Ernie from being charged by the police with culpable homicide, because Nell would surely have died.

However, my concern in relating this particular story is not just the victim and the perpetrator, for the influence of domestic violence on the workplace goes well beyond these two individuals. Many people at work become witnesses to the effects of domestic abuse, and there are times when we think that it is none of our business, that it is a matter to be sorted out by the family. But the profound traumatic impact that ripples through an organization when there is a discovery of abuse in an employee's home defies belief. As good citizens we cannot ignore the type of rage that causes domestic abuse. If we find out in the workplace that someone is violent in their own home, we really should protect ourselves from the influence of that violence. The likelihood of the violent person just restricting her or his outbursts to the home is small indeed. And who is to say that it will stop at the business's threshold?

We have already seen that there are various categories of perpetrators of workplace violence. Some of the most disturbing incidents for which I have had to provide response and support are ones in which the violence of the home life has spilled over into the workplace. As members of this society, we cannot turn our backs and ignore the fact that rage in the home can impact greatly on the workplace. We can choose to ignore the signs, the incremental behavioral changes, the bruises we see on our colleagues, the excuses (their out-of-the-blue propensity for "accidents"), the tangible fear expressed by the victim. But when we choose to keep quiet, we are making it possible for the cycle of violence to continue. Then we are really contributing to making our society, and not just our workplaces, unsafe. It is not always *someone else's job* to make changes. Sure, in Ernie's story, the supervisor took on the responsibility and is to be commended, but it does not always fall to people in perceived positions of responsibility to take steps to address rage and violence.

It takes individual courage to say, "Stop." It takes individual assertiveness to point out the discomfort with certain words and actions. It takes individual determination to be safe. It also takes guts. Of course, law and order have their place in making society safe, but the one thing we always have to remember is that society is not some globular entity. Our society consists entirely of individual, unique, freethinking persons. As such, each individual must surely adopt an attitude of responsibility for doing what he can to correct any behavior that is inappropriate and unacceptable, especially in the workplace. But then, a journey of a thousand miles begins with the first small step.

Chapter 7

Rage
and Robbery

When I joined the staff at Warren Shepell, I was surprised at how quickly I was spotted and targeted to take on responsibilities for trauma response. During the interview process, I was questioned regarding my experience of trauma, my readiness to respond and my ability to deal with what can often be "messy"—to put it mildly—tragedies.

At the end of orientation on the first week, a Friday afternoon, I was preparing to take up residence in my new office as a counselor and looking forward to the first day's clients. My new colleague, the person who managed the Trauma Response Service, asked me if I would accompany another colleague to a branch of a large bank where there had just been an armed robbery. We were to be at the bank on Monday morning, 8 a.m. sharp.

Monday morning came, and I was up at the crack of dawn, excited and gung-ho. It was going to be a long drive, so I left early to avoid traffic. Naturally, I got lost. Somewhere I managed to take a wrong turn, ended up on a quiet road that seemed to go nowhere and, being the stubborn male, would not have stopped to ask for directions—even if I could have found someone! Slowly, I began to panic. I meandered my way through the countryside, not really sure of my direction. To make a long story short, I arrived outside the bank at 7:59, the same moment my colleague stepped from her car and said, "You made it okay!" I wasn't traumatized, but I was anxious, sweating, hot and bothered. And that set the stage for my first debriefing in a bank setting—the first of many.

We entered the bank together, met the manager and the staff, and all of us adjourned upstairs to a large room where a group of comfortable chairs were set out in a circle. My mind was still on my lost journey to nowhere, but I was quickly brought back to earth as the staff, having been assured of confidentiality, unhurriedly began to recount their story of the robbery.

Because it was a small-town location, the tellers in that bank were badly affected by the robbery. Most bank robberies take place in large metropolitan areas, with easy access to transportation such as highways, subways and airports. The staff here, for the most part, had not been robbed before, and they felt a strong sense of personal violation. The robbers had violated their family territory. I use the word *family* deliberately. Most of the staff in the banks I have worked with liken their work group to a small family. They spend many years with each other and adopt some of the characteristics of a family system. They share openly; they argue openly; they have first-name relationships with their regular customers; they socialize together outside work—they sometimes spend more time with their colleagues than they do with their own families.

As they told the story of the robbery, the bank staff related it in a way that sounded as if a robber had come into their own home. I asked how many of them had been burglarized in their homes. From a group of about seven people, four of them had experienced a burglary, two of them during the previous six months, and one twenty years earlier. Their reactions to the bank robbery were identical to those experienced at the time of the burglary. Even the person who had been robbed all those years ago could remember in vivid detail not only what had happened, but how she had felt about it at the time. As they continued with their story, they became profoundly upset, shed many a tear and shared intimately the sense of helplessness they had felt at the hands of the perpetrators.

As mentioned earlier, more than 50 percent of our responses to workplace violence involve armed robbery. And I believe that figure is typical for North America; that is, about 50 percent of all workplace violence happens during armed robbery of banks, financial institutions, retail stores, gas bars and other businesses where cash changes hands.

Robbery violence is uncomplicated in one way: it is perpetrated by strangers to the work environment. When the robbery involves a stranger there is no existing relationship with the perpetrator and the tellers. Since no real connection is made, the chances of a quicker recovery are better than if the perpetrator is a colleague or a friend. But it is highly complicated in that it is life-threatening. Even if a gun or other weapon is not shown or declared on a note or in some other way, its presence is almost always implied. And there is no other type of violence, except terrorism, that produces such fear and terror. When someone is holding a gun to your head, or even if you believe a gun is present, your sense of danger is heightened. Add another robber or two, shouting of obscenities, physical pushing and shoving, and it is not surprising that when people are robbed at work, the only thing they really want to do after it is all over is return to the safety and security of home and family.

You Can Go Home Again

A couple of years ago, I received a call shortly after midnight. A swimming pool at a local municipality had been robbed. All the staff—a group in their late teens and early twenties—were upset. Would I please send out a counselor? When I diplomatically refused to send out a counselor, I was met with a torrent of misdirected rage. When I finally got the pool manager on the other end of the phone to calm down, I asked what it was she thought I could do for staff at that point. She responded, "Well, you know, tell them they're okay. You ought to know better than me!" Sure, I could get someone to go out and hold hands, and make the manager feel better. But in that situation, I explained, the physical shock of the robbery was probably just beginning to be felt, and she, as manager, could do just as good a job as a counselor. Her expectation was that a counselor would work a miracle, when I knew that the best approach was to get these young people home as quickly as possible. It would have been inappropriate to subject staff to a trauma counseling intervention, and they would have been annoyed at having to wait another hour for the arrival of a counselor—especially one who would only tell them they needed to feel safe at home. It's all a matter of education, that is, educating supervisors and leaders to know what to expect when people are traumatized, and how to be helpful to their staff. Sending for a counselor is not always the best approach.

Armed Robbery

In my own experience, the late 1990s has seen an upsurge in the use of weapons of all descriptions for robbery. When I began to work with my current employer, a great number of the robberies in banks, convenience stores, department stores and fast-food outlets were what we class as "simple robberies"; that is, if there was a weapon, it was concealed. Today, however, more and more weapons are appearing during robberies. Handguns, shotguns, machete knives, primitive bombs, even syringes full of HIV-infected blood—all are being used to intimidate the guardians of the cash. If this trend continues, steps must be taken by organizations to proactively minimize the risk of violence to employees who handle cash. Robberies are always going to occur, and employees, for their part, cannot delude themselves about the potential risks of their job. Employers need to remind staff regularly about those risks, so that staff can constantly be on the alert and put into practice the robbery prevention skills in which they are regularly trained.

Often after a robbery, when working with staff to mitigate traumatic impact, I get a sense that employees feel the need to blame their employer for putting their lives at risk. Even when every possible security measure is in place, staff still vent their anger at management. I believe this emotion is misdirected. Now, it is natural after a robbery for people to feel anger and rage; the response is normal for the abnormal situation. However, I often find myself wanting to remind staff that they work in a dangerous occupation. If anyone is to blame for the robbery, it is the robber, but because the robber is one step removed from the situation, management becomes the scapegoat. As a trauma responder, however, it is not always appropriate for me to say what I feel, or what I want. One of a crisis responder's most essential attributes is the ability to "be there" for the victims and witnesses, and that means setting aside personal agendas. Obviously, there are ways to get people to move from misdirected blame to directed blame, but it is more

88

important to begin by validating their feelings of blame, and letting them know such feelings are part of a normal reaction to the crisis.

I believe proactive education has to be offered on a regular basis for staff whose daily activities involve handling cash or other valuable items. And this education has to be both preventive and reactive.

Prevention

Any organization has to be concerned about making their facility safe and secure for employees. But in a bank or any kind of facility that handles cash, the security measures have to be directed toward making staff feel that they can protect themselves. So a robbery prevention program has to first address physical security. Here is a list of suggestions that might be helpful in strategic planning:

1. Ensure that the windows in the store, financial institution or place where money changes hands are clear of any kind of advertising and obstructions, so as to make the view inside and outside clear.
2. Position cash registers and teller points in areas where customers and outsiders, including patrolling police, can easily observe.
3. Make use of large signage, indicating that limited amounts of cash are kept on site. The same is true for drugs and other valuable items. A sign for this function has to be clear and prominently displayed. (A

small handwritten notice on the door will not
suffice.)

4. If the facility is a 24-hour operation, and an employee
is working alone, provide him or her with an easily
accessible list of emergency telephone numbers.

5. Make sure that the facility is well lit. Lighting should
be bright, both inside and outside.

These tips and many others can be part of a preventive
approach. But employees also need to be trained to
respond appropriately when robbery does occur.

Reactions

Recently, I had the pleasure of playing a small consulting
role in a video production sponsored by the Canadian
Banking Association. The new video was on a robbery
prevention program to be used by all the big banks in
Canada. My function was to observe staff being interviewed about their experiences of robbery during their
careers, to watch for recurring signs of trauma and to
debrief the staff at the conclusion. For me, it was a very
interesting and worthwhile process. The interviewer and
the camera operators did a great job of relaxing the interviewees and making them feel comfortable in recounting
their stories. I sat and observed the interviews in the
company of a staff consultant from one of the large
banks. We were mesmerized as the stories unfolded,
delighted with the responses given, and speechless at the
candor with which these victims offered advice to

colleagues in all banks about what to do when faced with a robbery.

The advice was on how to react during a robbery, and how to retain a sense of well-being, control and safety. All the interviewees used similar words, and the completed video, which I recently previewed, reflects the simple, sound and practical advice suitable for people in any robbery situation. It came down to three words: Stop, Look, Listen. I am convinced that all managers and supervisors and those who have responsibility for safety and security can teach the following three steps to any employee who may be at risk due to handling money, or drugs or other valuable commodities.

Stop

When you are faced with a robber, the most important thing you can do is give him your attention. All sorts of things are flying through your mind at the time, everything from worrying about family to "What can I do to stop my colleagues from being hurt?" It is important to get into "self-talk" mode and say clearly inside your head, "Stop!" Your body will be telling you to run away, to faint, to obstruct, to scream, but you must tell yourself to stop.

Gently and calmly take a few deep breaths; allow the oxygen to circulate again through your system. That will help you control your thinking, and get your body prepared for action.

Look

Be prepared to look at the robber—observe, but do not stare. Try not to let your mind jump ahead to think about where the gun might be, or what he might do with the gun. Look him in the eye, if not directly, then as close as you are able. He needs to know that you are going to cooperate, and the way to make him aware of this is to look at him. Let him see that you are ready to do as he says.

Listen

Pay attention to what the robber is saying. Listen to him, and make sure he knows you are listening. Still breathing gently, calmly, deeply, and mastering control of the moment, follow through on the listening by doing what he tells you to do. Remember that by doing so, you are acting safely, and thus ensuring the safety of colleagues and customers who may also be present.

Once the robber leaves the facility, you can allow yourself to do, think, feel whatever you want. But for those moments that he is in your space, it is crucial that you maintain control. If you have these three little words—Stop, Look, Listen—as a slogan, ready to use when necessary, you will avoid freezing during a holdup, and the possible life-threatening complications that can arise as a result.

The Kidd Killing
Early in 1999, for the first time in living memory, a staff

member in a Canadian bank was murdered during an armed robbery. Nancy Kidd, a long-term employee of the Toronto-Dominion Bank, a wife and mother of two grown-up children, was shot and killed while she lay on the floor in a corner of the branch, corralled with her colleagues. She had been doing what she had been ordered by the robbers to do, and yet she was murdered. No one will ever be able to provide sufficient explanation to her husband and family as to why this happened. No one will be able to understand the complexity of their grief and loss, nor that of the community where she lived and worked, nor that of the extended banking community. We are left with a deeply grieving family, slowly trying to rebuild their lives; with a shaken community, aghast to have experienced such tragedy; with a regretful banking industry, struggling to make things as safe as possible for their staff, and yet apprehensive about the future.

The repercussions of such a tragedy are widespread and long-lasting. Everyone who hears the news and who has to face the prospect of handling money in their job, most of whom do so to fulfill that need we all have for daily bread and shelter, will experience worry and anxiety. How can we stop such robberies? To this question I have no reply. I believe the problem is rooted in much larger societal issues than I can begin to deliberate here. In Nancy Kidd's case, two suspected villains were apprehended, and we can only hope that the criminal justice system delivers justice in a way that allows closure for the Kidd family, the bank staff and the surrounding community.

Money has always been an easy, and tempting, target for theft. If I were to offer one small piece of advice to all those who handle money in their jobs, it would be this: Never try to be a hero. Human life is far more valuable than money. *Star Trek* fans will recognize the quote "Resistance is futile!" In a robbery situation, resistance is futile—and potentially fatal.

Chapter 8

Rage
in the Skies

In July 1999 Canada's Airports initiated a campaign to
address the problem of "air rage." In the news reports
that accompanied the start of this campaign, the International Air Transport Association publicly acknowledged
that there has been a 400 percent increase in incidents of
air rage since 1995, mainly affecting the United States,
with a smaller percentage increase here in Canada. And
the Minister of Transport, in an effort to support the
airline industry and to ensure passenger safety, has
declared that there will be zero tolerance for rage in the
skies.

Abusive and unruly behavior by airline passengers is a global problem. The goal of this
campaign is to heighten awareness that interfer-
ence with crew members is unacceptable, and
that we together with our partners, have a zero-
tolerance for such behavior. Through this

campaign, we are demonstrating our commitment
to ensuring the safety of crew and passengers.

Minister of Transport

I am a frequent flyer, at times flying five or six times a month. I do consider myself to have been fortunate, in that I have not witnessed any major disaster in the skies. Sure, the normal turbulence and resulting buffeting have at times been alarming and frightening, but I now consider that to be part and parcel of having to move about the country regularly. The closest I ever got to a rage situation happened on the ground while preparing for the takeoff, and it involved one of the most common situations that people in the airline industry now have to worry about, the case of the belligerent drunk.

In fact, the case of a drunk was one that became very famous in 1996 when one Gerard Finnerman, a successful U.S. businessman, went berserk when he was refused another drink by a flight attendant. Finnerman somehow managed to get hold of a service cart, climbed on top, dropped his pants and relieved himself in the middle of the aisle! Not a pretty sight I'm sure for those around the scene, and for Mr. Finnerman who was subsequently arrested!

The case I witnessed was not so extraordinary. The flight that day bound for Scotland happened to be delayed by a few hours. During the wait, a few people were becoming a bit rowdy in the bar area of the departure lounge. Three people in particular seemed to be a bit louder than everyone else—they were singing and shouting and appeared to be a bit merrier than others sitting sipping quietly at their drinks. By the time the plane was being boarded it became clear that one of the three was plainly drunk and disorderly. As I sat and watched the three of them I began to think that it would be just my luck to have them sitting beside me on the aircraft for the next seven hours. And sure as the fates allow, that's what happened.

When we boarded the plane my loudmouthed traveling companions sat in the three seats directly behind me. Our plane sat at the gate for a while as the passengers boarded. People in the neighboring seats exchanged glances as they watched and listened and fretted at the hopelessness of the situation: no one wanted to sit and listen to that racket continuously for seven hours!

Just a couple of minutes before the aircraft door was closed over and locked, a group of flight attendants appeared in the aisle. One of them spoke up loudly for all to hear. "Sir," she said, "there has been a complaint. We are here to ask you to leave the aircraft." Her message was directed only to the one who was the loudest and most abusive. There was a torrent of foul language, and a fierce argument broke out. Eventually, the obnoxious inebriate was escorted from the plane by the captain, first officer and the flight attendants. Everyone sighed with relief—even his two friends, who were allowed to remain on the plane.

Fortunately, this story ended well, but matters could

easily have gotten out of hand. The stupidity of one traveler can put an entire planeload of people at risk. We know that the rage of the inebriate is among the worst kinds of rage. Who can argue with a drunk and win? He has no reasoning power available. "Drinking" leads to "stinking thinking"—and the outcome is often violent. I relate this story to highlight the potential danger that flight attendants and other airline staff face on a regular basis. In this instance, the staff were able to address the situation prior to takeoff, and ensure a positive outcome for themselves and for the rest of the passengers. But what about the next time, when staff have to deal with a customer's rage at 40,000 feet?

Frequently we hear stories in the media about the challenges facing airline staff. In one very recent situation in December 1999, we heard of two people on a flight to Montreal who were so drunk that the plane was forced to abandon its plans to take off. The two people put up a great struggle as they were escorted from the plane by the police. And this is not such an isolated incident. In another story also from December 1999, a man on a flight to Mexico became so abusive he assaulted another passenger. It took eight people to hold him down and two doses of valium, administered by a doctor on the flight, to get him calmed down. In another incident that hit the press in the summer of 1999, a couple of people became so intoxicated that they allowed their behavior to become really inappropriate—they started to have sex openly in their seats on the plane. However, not all of the stories hit the media. Since I travel a lot by air I always get opportunities to ask flight attendants for their own "war stories" and I never cease to be amazed at what I hear. On one recent flight an attendant told me that he had been physically assaulted when he discovered a passenger smoking and tried to get him to put out the cigarette. This passenger became enraged and so aggressive that he hit out at the flight attendant. The same flight attendant also told me that his colleagues have catalogues of such tales of woe.

Given that the demand for air transportation has been steadily increasing over the years, I suspect that it will continue to expand as the world develops and borders open up. In all likelihood, we'll see more rage in the skies, too.

Where does this particular rage originate? I have a few ideas on the subject, and include them here as a start to the dialogue.

- Many rage situations in aircraft happen as a direct result of individuals *overindulging in alcohol*. It is well known that high-altitude pressurization causes dehydration. When you combine alcohol, in itself a diuretic, with a system that is already low on liquids, the body will begin to react badly. Drunkenness takes effect more quickly. That means that the individual's ability to think clearly and coherently diminishes. Personal safety is then compromised, as is the safety of other travelers. One way to counteract this is for flight attendants to provide safety awareness education at the beginning of the flight, at the same time as they provide other safety demonstrations. As a Canadian and a Scot, I would not like to suggest a ban on alcohol consumption during flights. A wee gin and tonic on a long flight can work wonders for the appetite. However, I do believe people have to be reminded of certain basic truths, one of which is that there is a direct correlation between high blood-alcohol levels and overt expressions of aggression.

- The flight crew's primary function is to ensure the safety of the aircraft and the passengers. Yet many passengers have become *complacent about the need for safety*. They are more interested in the fact that they need a pillow, and show little respect for the fact that the flight attendant also has responsibility for attending to safety during the flight. Flying, although one of the safest forms of transportation, is still a risky business. It demands that we pay attention to safety first.

- Aggression, outbursts of rage and violent behavior often occur as a result of *stress*. For example, being delayed in an airport can be extremely frustrating for both passengers and crew alike. But when there is no explanation for the delay, except for the fact that the incoming flight is delayed, people become agitated. The longer the delay, the more need there is for communication. Airlines in the past have not been very open and honest in their communication, and this is easy to understand—how many people would really want to know that the incoming aircraft had suffered an engine malfunction, when they are expected to fly out in the same aircraft? So in order to avoid unnecessary panic, I'm sure, airlines vet every communication to the waiting public. And no, I do not want to give the impression that the airline's lack of communication is an excuse for an outburst of rage on the part of the passenger; being stressed is no excuse for turning violent. But an airline's effort to communicate information at least eases anxiety for travelers. I'm happy to say that the last time I suffered a flight delay, we were updated every few minutes on the status of the flight and the reasons for the delay—and this was a pleasant surprise. But it was also unique!

It would be naïve and simplistic to suggest that alcohol consumption, complacency and delay-stress are the only causes of rage in the skies. But they certainly are contributing factors. There are also other contributing factors, including the fact that some people who get onto planes are also people who can be violent persons, fitting some of the parameters of the profile we talked about earlier in this book. Prevention of rage in the skies in this scenario can be difficult to maintain. In order to prevent rage, a certain amount of training and education of airline staff will be necessary to heighten their awareness of the signs of disruptive behavior in people as they check in for their flight or as they board the aircraft. And as well as training of staff, the members of the public who fly also have to be trained in the airlines' policies of zero tolerance for abuse, disruptive behavior and the legal action that will ensue for any action that will endanger airline staff or members of the flying public.

Chapter 9

Dealing with Difficult People

I "explode" so seldom that I can remember exactly the last time it happened. April 1985. And I feel as badly about the incident today as I did then.

During my years of existential angst as a priest, I was always obliged to live in someone else's home. Usually, I was provided with a bed-sitting room, like a small bachelor's pad, and that was where I spent most of the time when not out and about performing the priestly functions relating to "hatches, matches and dispatches." Meals were provided and presented by the live-in housekeeper, a person hired by the parish priest to look after the normal household needs of three unrelated grown men. The housekeeper—let's call her Helga—during the period I'm referring to was explosive.

It's strange to look back at some of the bizarre behavior she presented to the people of the parish who sought spiritual solace: slamming doors in their faces, throwing the telephone down in fits of rage. She was a dichotomy, indeed. One day she would be out feeding the beggars in the foyer of our home, demonstrating the essence of Christian charity, and the next she'd be screaming blue murder at us. She was hilariously funny at times, mad as a hatter at others.

During the first few years of my assignment, I established a fairly good relationship with her, making sure I kept out of her way during the bad times. As time passed, though, and as I was struggling with my continued unhappiness with life as a priest, our relationship deteriorated. At the beginning of 1985, we ceased communicating entirely. This is not a normal pattern of behavior for me!

During those months, I sought help from a number of sources inside the priesthood, colleagues, friends, confessors, many of whom encouraged me to stay put, and not to leave my post. The lack of open communication in the home just added to my feeling of hypocrisy: I was trying to be a spiritual role model for the people in the parish, and yet I couldn't string together two kind words for our *Hausfrau*.

Along came the Easter Triduum, the three Holy Days of the Easter Season in the Catholic Church. Holy Thursday is a special day for priests, one on which the institution of the priesthood is celebrated. To put it plainly, on Holy Thursday, priests are allowed to celebrate the fact that they are priests. I did not feel very much like celebrating anything that day, never mind the fact that I was contemplating life after the Church! I came walking out of my little room upstairs, and started descending the staircase. At the same moment, Helga began walking up toward me. At the corner, where one flight ended and the other began, she lifted her head and saw me coming down, then immediately turned on her heels and started running down the stairs!

Well, the dam burst. I totally lost it. I was the one doing the screaming. All the rage poured out and it hit her in the face—not physically, I hasten to add, only verbally. My colleagues heard the commotion from within the dining room, popped their heads out the door, then, upon seeing me venting, quickly hid again. (I would like to think that they were cheering me on!) The housekeeper could not keep her mouth shut, either. Out from her came a torrent of abuse, the kind of bottled-up nonsense that means nothing when you think about it later. I have no idea how long it lasted or what was said. But I do remember eventually kissing and hugging and making up with her. For then! Since it was Holy Thursday, I did celebrate, but what I celebrated was a decision. If I could not get out of the priesthood, I would, at least, get out of *there*. Three months later, I volunteered for a new assignment in another town. (And that was the beginning of another story, related earlier, the one about the Bully. Talk about out of the frying pan into the fire!)

Difficult Customers

Since those early days in my career, I have learned much about dealing with difficult people. There are many of them around, and they exert great influence in the workplace. Dissatisfied customers are the greatest source of aggravation to customer service representatives all over the country. Customers seem to see it as their right to treat the person on the other side of the counter or on the other end of the line with disrespect. In many customer service environments, I hear horror stories about the things customers say on the phone—the abusive language, racial slurs, sexual innuendo and suggestive remarks, as well as the aggressive comments and threats. No one should be expected to accept that kind of behavior. How we behave and what we accept as appropriate in our own homes is our own business, but how we behave and what we have to accept in our workplaces does not include abuse, whether verbal, physical or emotional.

Communication

Communication is highly complex, involving factors you identify with your senses, as well as all the invisible codes and signals that have been conveyed from generation to generation through our genetic make-up. For example, when we are flirting, how do we know if the signals we are getting back are favorable or unfavorable? Do we have a sense of smell, above and beyond the normal, that is unconsciously arousing and therefore helping us along in our courting behavior? Or is it all a matter of consciously reading the signs and fretting over a nod of the head, a twist of the finger? It's all so complicated.

In human communication patterns, there are three general methods by which people express themselves:

- **Assertive:** in control but not domineering
- **Nonassertive:** laid back or timid
- **Aggressive:** overbearing and threatening

There are also three components to the complete communication process:

- **Verbal:** the words that we use
- **Nonverbal:** the use of the body in the process
- **Meta-language:** the way in which the words are delivered

When dealing with difficult customers, especially if they are aggressive, it is important always to be on the assertive side of communication. Don't let the aggressor walk all over you, and then *you* apologize! In that type of scenario, you will lose ground and become angry, and the aggressive person will make you feel bad about yourself. The key to successfully handling difficult customers lies in your ability to communicate assertively.

We hear lots today about the use of body language in the workplace, about "reading" the body language of colleagues and about presenting "positive" body language while we work. Interesting research has been conducted for more than 20 years by Desmond Morris, a famous zoologist from England. His insights are fascinating, especially his comparisons between the animal kingdom and human beings. A group I worked with recently were convinced that because I happened to mention this subject during a workshop on stress management, I must have been in cahoots with their managers. They had recently received information from management, too, on negative body-language images. In fact, I normally include a segment on communication techniques when I lecture on stress management, since I firmly believe that a lot of workplace stress is a result of poor communication.

Assertive Communication

As a guideline, when having to face the ordeal of handling a difficult customer or client, be a good listener. In the workplace, it has become fashionable to teach everyone, especially management, how to be an empathetic listener. Empathy is the listening skill by which you convey to the other person your understanding of their situation. It also includes an ability to be able to sense and reflect back in a clarifying manner what the other senses.

The famous psychologist Carl Rogers, the father of nondirective, client-centered therapy, indicates in his works that people who really want to be empathetic listeners have to be securely grounded in their own world. In entering what can be the bizarre world of "the other," a person cannot afford to be lost—he or she must be able to return to their own world at will. This approach can work extremely well in therapy, but not necessarily in the workplace. There is every possibility that the world of the aggressor may seem to the average listening person to be extremely strange. An empathetic approach to the aggression may turn out to be dangerous for the listener, especially if the listener is not aware of the principles of transference and counter-transference. The listener can be drawn into the aggression, and in turn feed it right back to the aggressor. It makes more sense to me to take a middle-of-the-road approach, to strike a balance between an empathetic listening approach and a directive approach.

Interestingly, when I was working as a full-time therapist and counselor, I was always slightly amused by the number of people who *wanted* the directive approach to counseling. The directive approach is almost an advice-giving mode of therapy. Advice-giving was never my preference in therapy, since my counseling training had been mainly Rogerian. I was much more interested in trying to get the client to see counseling as a process of self-determination.

In dealing with a difficult and aggressive customer, in person or on the phone, it is important to be able to listen empathetically, but it is also vital to be at times directive, especially at moments when you sense a situation of abusive conflict. You must be able to call the shots! The person who is being aggressive must understand that the aggression is inappropriate and unwanted, and that you, as the listener, will not accept such behavior. The listener has to be able to say, for example,

"When you swear at me, you make me feel uncomfortable. I need you to stop in order to be able to help you." In making such a statement, you are being empathetic in reflecting back the frightening attitude of the aggressor. You let her or her know of the discomfort you feel, and you are *directive* in requesting that they cease the behavior. This approach to dealing with a difficult customer can often defuse the situation. Try using the following model:

When you....................(*describe the action*)
I feel.......................(*describe your reaction*)
I need..........................(*require that it cease*)

As well as using the empathetic/directive approach to listening, there are a number of other ways in which a person can communicate more assertively. These involve the style of delivery of the words—the meta-language and body language. Below are a few examples of delivery techniques reflecting the more assertive approach to dealing with a difficult customer. The first few indicate techniques for a controlled voice; the remainder, techniques for reflecting a controlled body.

Intonation

The assertive communicator is the one who uses a tone of voice that sounds relaxed, but in control. This means that sentences should sound as if they are statements, not questions. Many Canadians have a habit of ending sentences on an up-beat, making it sound like a question. Being assertive means showing that you are controlled, even if inside you feel like Jell-O. Try making your statement end on a down-beat. It promotes the notion of being in control.

Speed

In assertive communication, it's important to keep the speed of your conversation under control. If you speak quickly, there is the possibility that you will be misunderstood, and if you speak too slowly, you are likely to sound banal and patronizing. It can be difficult to know your own speed, so if you are in any doubt, ask a friend or a colleague to listen and let you know.

Pitch

People with high-pitched voices often sound timid, and people with deep pitch can sound aggressive. To be assertive, you need to have a pitch of voice that is neither high nor deep. When Margaret Thatcher became prime minister of the United Kingdom, she took a series of elocution lessons to learn how to drop the pitch of her voice. Prior to the election, she had a very high-pitched, tinny voice, and within months she developed a more media-friendly pitch, which helped her create an impression of being in control, and gave credibility to her statements.

Volume

Similarly, if you speak too quietly, you can sound timid, and if you speak too loudly, you can sound aggressive. The assertive person is neither quiet nor loud, but can be heard with ease by the listener.

Facial Expression

The face says it all, and most of the time we have the freedom to express there our deepest fears and greatest joys. But in a potentially aggressive situation, the listener must be careful not to reveal inner feelings. An assertive person should look attentive, concerned, but not exaggerated in any way. The face has to depict "controlled authenticity."

Posture

When you go into your manager's office and you find feet up on the desk, body laid back in the chair, arms behind the head, what kind of message does this convey? Or if you find the manager sitting on the edge of a chair, leaning forward, looking ready to pounce, what does this convey? Our bodies send signals to other people, but sometimes the signals can be misconstrued. When confronted by an aggressive customer, you need to radiate a look of relaxed confidence through your posture. Back straight, shoulders up, chest out—all the things we were taught as children about the proper way to present ourselves can be important in signaling to the aggressor that you are not intimidated.

Hand Gestures

Hands should only be used when necessary, and only to highlight a point that you are trying to make. Obviously, cultural differences reign supreme in this area as in so many others. For example, ask a person with Italian ancestry to stop using her hands in conversation, and all you'll get is silence! Hand gestures can speak volumes. For example, pointing a finger in someone's face is often perceived as an aggressive act, whereas using the hands in an open way, palms facing upward, is perceived as nonthreatening. It says, "I have nothing to hide!"

Body Tone

Try not to fidget with pens or paperclips, make unnecessary hand movements, fold the arms, cross or uncross the legs. When people do these things, they appear nervous. To be assertive, you have to look relaxed, but exude an air of confidence. Of course, if you are dealing with an aggressor on the telephone, your body tone will not by visible, although a good one can boost your own confidence level and help you to be more assertive.

Eye Contact

In North American culture, the assertive person maintains strong eye contact. However, eye contact is a personal, intimate behavior. The norms of other cultures dictate differently; for some, it's considered confrontational or challenging. In dealing with an aggressive or difficult customer, therefore, it is important to be sensitive to the cultural differences that make our diverse Canadian society the wonder that it is.

These elements of assertive communication are not to be considered hard-and-fast rules. There are always going to be times when misunderstandings and conflicts arise in communication that have no relationship to a person's ability to be assertive, and to do with who they are, what they are experiencing at that time, their upbringing and culture and a host of other factors. The assertive communicator faced with the difficult customer has many things to think about simultaneously. We have probably all experienced, at one time or another, the "customer from hell"—the demanding, confrontational, negative and abusive person who adheres to the motto "The customer is always right." In such cases, it is a must that we display assertiveness in our words, actions and attitudes. However, what in one culture may be perceived as assertiveness, in another may be perceived as arrogance. The dividing line between the two is thin. Remember, a high level of cultural awareness will serve you well.

Cultural Awareness and Self-Awareness

The first rule about other-culture awareness has its roots in self-awareness. To become aware of another's culture is commendable, but it will not be useful unless one has established an understanding of one's own preconceived beliefs and ideas. The best way to uncover those preconceptions is to put yourself to the test. The next time you are out driving on the highway, and someone makes what you consider to be a wrong move, stop and think about the first thing that comes to mind. Do you think, *Typical woman driver*, or something equally prejudicial? Is this type of thinking spontaneous and based only on chauvinistic societal thinking about female drivers, or is it based on your deep-seated conviction that men are more powerful and therefore better than women? This shows a built-in bigotry and a preconceived notion about the place of women in society, and can unconsciously infiltrate our day-to-day thoughts and actions. I hope the reader will forgive me for using the example of the female driver, but it is one that plays out every day and is easily perpetuated.

Become aware of your own preconceived opinions before setting out on a journey of cross-cultural awareness. In recognizing our own individuality, you can better recognize others as individual and unique.

Cultural Interest

As a multicultural nation, Canada has an opportunity to show the rest of the world that multiculturalism can succeed. However, I sometimes think we make so much of the theory that we forget the practice. Again, it's a situation of not walking the talk. Many people in the workplace are given opportunities to attend seminars and workshops dealing with respect, harassment, discrimination and race relations. But I wonder how many of those workshops actually serve any useful purpose for those participating? For most adults, hearing is one thing; real learning through interactive participation—learning from each other—is another.

One of the best ways to promote multiculturalism is to promote interest in cultural diversity. This can be accomplished fairly easily by sharing information on the practices associated with birth and family, marriage, death and other significant life events. When people share information about the significance of customs and rituals, understanding grows, and so too, often, does admiration. When employees have the occasion to celebrate life events outside of work, the exchange of information inside of work on various cultural norms can be enlightening. And enlightened people do not as easily slip into prejudicial and biased ways of thinking, which in turn can lead to acts of discrimination.

So how does this help when you are faced with a raging customer? Enlightened people also tend to be more tolerant people, who will not slip into defensive thinking patterns when confronted with aggression.

Cultural Positivity

When I am teaching people about respect in the workplace, I often relate to them some stories about cultural life in my native Scotland. For example, I talk about the rituals surrounding death and burial, and how some of the observances may seem strange to a North American hearing about them for the first time. One of the reasons I use such examples is to help people understand that one culture is not better than another—it is just different. My explanation of death rites in Scotland opens up the topic so the class can share and discuss the fact that we all have different death rites. Some may be perceived as obscure, others bizarre, some beautiful and others scary. We are each different, but different does not indicate superior or inferior.

I present my cultural heritage in a positive light, at the same time encouraging others to present theirs likewise. But I am not trying to suggest that the Scottish way is the best way. I am trying to help participants understand some of the meaning around the rituals, many of which continue on though their meaning is lost in history.

Another example is that of "arranged" marriages. Many North Americans would find the idea of having a marriage arranged by parents very unusual, or even weird. We would immediately think of the *negative* aspects of this cultural norm, primary among them being the fact that the chosen partners are denied freedom of choice for life and love. This as an example of an area in which we jump to prejudicial conclusions due to our lack of understanding. But how might an arranged marriage be presented in a *positive* light so the average North American would understand it? When people get to the point of listening to and understanding another culture positively, then problematic behavior associated with prejudice begins to dissipate.

One last thought on employee versus aggressive customer: sometimes you have to take a step back. When you seem to be dealing with aggression on a regular basis from customers, clients or even colleagues, and nothing seems to stop it, you have to take a step back. As objectively as you can, ask yourself if your own behavior is adding fuel to the fire. Are you being perceived as timid, assertive or aggressive? Would you even be able to recognize yourself by someone else's description? We all know that there are occasions when our own inaction or zealousness adds to a problem at work. Maybe—just maybe—there are also times when what we hear and see in an aggressive customer reflects what that customer hears and sees in us.

Chapter 10

Rage
and Trauma

In April 1999, one week after the massacre at Columbine High School in Littleton, Colorado, in which 13 people were killed, in the small town of Taber, Alberta, a 14-year-old boy carried out a "copycat" killing in his former W.R. Myers High School. He went to school with a .22 calibre sawn-off rifle and shot two of his schoolmates. One of them, Jason Lang, the 17-year-old son of a local clergyman, died instantly and the other, also 17, was seriously wounded. The people of Taber, having witnessed the intrusiveness of the media in Littleton, expressed that they wanted privacy to mourn their loss.

I was sitting in my car one evening, waiting outside the train station for the arrival of a friend whom I was picking up. Over the radio came news of tragic shooting at a high school in Taber, Alberta. I felt profoundly saddened on two counts. First, this incident in Taber brought back memories of a few years earlier, when there had been an awful abduction and homicide of a convenience-store owner in this same small town. I felt sure that old wounds would be reopened. Second, it seemed to me that it had only been about a week since the killings in Columbine High School in Littleton, Colorado, when students had gone on a rampage with guns, killing several young people and a teacher, and terrifying others. The Taber incident was described on the radio as a copycat killing modeled after the event at Columbine.

When the news bulletin ended, I listened to a related call-in show, during which members of the public were given the opportunity to state their views to a prominent and oft-times controversial radio commentator. As the opinions of the presenter became clear, I found myself feeling more and more disturbed. I was actually on the point of picking up my phone and calling in to the show myself. In talking about the experiences of the families in Taber, he said that everyone ought to leave the families alone to process the grief and the trauma of the event. At one point he said something like this: "Taber does not need social workers or grief counselors or any kind of professional help. Just leave them alone. They don't need a bandwagon of do-gooders popping out psychobabble."

What was troublesome about such advice was that it showed no knowledge of or respect for the profound traumatic impact that such an event can have on an entire town, not to mention the high school community itself.

Why have I put this short episode to paper? It has been my experience that the impact of trauma on victims, witnesses and communities at large is vastly underestimated, and this is particularly true in the event of tragedy resulting from rage and violence. Every appropriate source of help should be made available to people affected by trauma of any kind. A radio personality perpetrating a myth that families can go it alone does nothing to assist the recovery process for the many victims of trauma. It can be true that when there is a large-scale disaster, a deluge of well-intentioned therapists follow who want to offer assistance and support to the victims. But this is often the response to a request for help by leaders of the community where the tragedy occurs. I do not know of any therapist who would pitch a tent at the scene of a tragedy, seeking out business!

Trauma Response Service

I often tell people that the Trauma Response Service, which I am proud to lead, does not engage in "ambulance-chasing." We do not go in search of work, but wait until requested to provide support, and then do so to the best of our ability. The work that is carried out in Trauma Response is never intended to replace family support. While we hope that the outcome of our work will be openness in families that can help each other, we have to be cognizant of the fact that for our society—a multiracial, multicultural and multireligious society—the word *family* has a wide variety of connotations. Not everyone belongs to a classic "nuclear" family, with two parents and 2.2 children and extended family, such as grandparents, aunts, uncles and cousins.

When a tragedy occurs in the workplace, I firmly believe, the employer is duty-bound, if not legally then morally, to make sure that employees have access to appropriate mechanisms of support. A supportive intervention will take into account the actual needs, background, lifestyle and coping abilities of the employees. When we are assessing the requirements of an organization after a tragedy, there are a number of areas we investigate, so that we can be well briefed and prepared to be as supportive as possible.

In the first instance, we obviously try to find out if the tragedy that has occurred fits the definition of *tragedy*. Specialists in trauma response consider a tragedy to be a sudden unexpected event, life-threatening or at least life-altering in some way, which has emotionally overwhelmed those involved. A trauma, particularly a situation of violence, is not something you would expect to encounter every day. Similarly, since it is an abnormal event or series of events, the feelings associated with it are very disturbing to the victims and witnesses. And as well as being overwhelmed, the victims experience some element of threat to life. Falling down the stairs and breaking a leg is not what I would objectively describe, in trauma response terms, as a "traumatic experience." However, being held up in a bank with a gun pointed at your head certainly fits the definition: it's sudden, over-whelming and life-threatening.

Following this first-stage assessment, we then consider five other factors that contribute to the impact a trauma has on people.

Severity

We know that each individual witnessing the same event will have a different perception of what actually happened. So we have to obtain an objective perception in order to understand how severe the event has been. For example, a simple note-passing bank robbery is entirely different from a robbery involving multiple robbers, sawed-off shotguns, hostage-taking, kicking, shouting, violent language and abuse. Following the former, people probably will recover fairly quickly, but following the latter, the recovery period will be much longer.

Duration

A tragedy that lasts only a few seconds can have profound impact, but one that lasts for days or weeks can be devastating. For example, when an airplane is bombed out of the skies by terrorists, the search and recovery can take days upon days. Meanwhile, all the family members are waiting for the actual death notification to take place, something that can only happen upon identification of the human remains. The duration for this event will be as long as it takes to bring closure through death notifica-tion. The longer it takes, the more traumatized the family members may be. The ripple effect for this type of trauma is incredible, encompassing the many thousands of people who make an honest living by working for the many airlines around the world. An attack on an airline is the ultimate workplace violence.

Suddenness
In some disaster situations, there is a warning period. For example, when there is a tropical storm in the Caribbean, the entire eastern seaboard of North America gets into preparation mode. But some tragedies happen totally out of the blue. Bank robbery, a shooting at work, a death threat, harassment to the point of physical harm—all of these tend to be sudden, and so we are unprepared for them. The more sudden the event, the more profound will be the traumatic reaction.

Ability to understand
People like us have a habit of trying to find meaning in the many life events that come our way. When we are able to comprehend events and situations, we find a much clearer way to integrate the events with day-to-day living. They become almost part of our make-up as people. It's one of the features that distinguishes us from the animal kingdom—that is, our spirituality, our ability to ponder origins, evolution, living and dying. When assessing the impact of an act of violence at the workplace, I often enquire about the search for understanding that occurs among groups of people affected by the

tragedy. The better people can understand the event, the better their ability to cope in the aftermath.

For example, people can reach a level of understanding about a junkie who robs a bank to feed the drug habit. But can the same people understand why someone would murder a colleague at work and then commit suicide? The intentionality of the latter act is less clear. Our ability to comprehend is diminished, and the less we are able to understand, the more time we will take to recover.

Survivor Stability

In this final assessment, we try to find out whether the particular group of people we have been asked to support has experienced anything untoward in the recent past. One traumatic experience can trigger memories of another experience from the past, either consciously or unconsciously. When I am doing a workshop on training in trauma response procedures, I often say at this point that determining stability of survivor equilibrium at the time of the event means asking, "Were you having a bad day, anyway?" Or to put it another way, asking, "Is there anything else going on in your life at the moment that would hinder your natural instinct to cope and recover?"

When dealing with a group affected by the violence of co-workers or strangers to the workplace, it can be difficult to find out enough about the private and personal experiences of the individuals. But if managers or supervisors are hands-on people, they probably will be able to provide the trauma response counselor with information about family backgrounds, divorce situations, custody battles, parenting issues, elder care, recent illness, and other situations that might impede the normal recovery from trauma.

People who suffer the indignity and trauma of violence at work experience a wide range of reactions, all of them "normal reactions to an abnormal situation." The situation is clearly abnormal, because of the sudden, overwhelming and dangerous components that we considered above. But the reactions to the situation are predictable. Most of the research in the area of trauma has been carried out on victims of violence, particularly with the victims of war and its associated atrocities. Traumatic reaction to violence is a worldwide phenomenon, and the types of reactions indicated in the research are experienced by people of every social class, every level of intelligence and understanding, every cultural and religious background and every age group. Reactions are generally broken down into the following four distinct groupings:

- Reactions that affect the physical body
- Reactions of an emotional nature
- Reactions affecting the ability to think
- Reactions affecting behavior

Trauma Reactions
Physical Reactions

- Heart rate increase associated with adrenaline rush
- Physical shock, tremors, shaking
- Hyperventilation
- Sense of being frozen in place; inability to move
- Headaches
- Appetite swings, from starving to comfort eating
- Jettison effect; the body may void
- Dehydration
- Disorientation
- Heightened sensory perception: hearing, touch, taste, smell
- Physical arousal

Emotional Reactions
First Stage—Emotional Shock

- Shock
- Disbelief
- Denial: *"I can't believe this is happening to me."*

Second Stage—Flood of Feelings

- Anger, sometimes feelings of rage
- Sadness at the losses involved, especially if there is violent death
- Frustration at being helpless

- Irritability at everyone, including uninvolved family
- Withdrawal from social circle
- Lack of interest in intimacy and sex
- Guilt and self-blame: "*It's all my fault!*"
- Confusion: "*Why did it happen?*"
- Fear of a recurrence: "*Will it happen again?*"

Third Stage—Restoring Balance
- Acceptance
- Equilibrium
- Sense of finding meaning
- New normal; nothing is ever the same again

Thinking Reactions
- Concentration problems
- Difficulties making decisions
- Poor attention span and poor short-term memory
- Distraction
- Daydreams
- Making small mistakes
- Repetition of completed tasks
- Flashbacks to the scene

Behavioral Reactions
- Tendency to either stay off work or overwork
- Drop in productivity
- Cyclical conversation

- Drop in team spirit
- Development of rigid patterns, or disappearance of patterns altogether
- Tendency to treat people with suspicion, especially in a "customer" setting
- Hypersensitivity to peer comments
- Promiscuity or self-medication with alcohol, drugs

Trauma Intervention

The focus of attention in trauma response intervention is the normalization of the reactions described above. This is carried out by a competent and trained therapist in a group setting, bringing together the victims and witnesses of the tragedy. Whether the tragedy is a sudden death at work or a co-worker's violent episode, trauma intervention is designed to initiate the recovery process for all those affected by the experience. There are several types of trauma intervention, each designed with a similar purpose and generally following a similar pattern. The name given to these interventions is trauma *debriefing*.

Debriefing is a word we hear a lot today, and it is used in many different contexts. People say, "We need to debrief." The term is used to indicate a revisiting of something that has happened in the past. In trauma therapy, debriefing is used as a means to revisit the emotional impact experienced by those affected in any way by the tragedy. Likewise, it is also used as a means to prepare and educate the affected as to what may be in store for them in the coming days, weeks and even months ahead. Debriefing is a powerful tool in trauma psychology. I have facilitated many hundreds of trauma debriefings, and I never cease to be amazed at the intensity of emotional expression and cathartic healing that accompanies the process.

Since the field of trauma response in its infancy, the effectiveness of the debriefing process itself has been questioned. Traditionally, in any kind of research in medicine, science, pharmacology and even psychology, effectiveness and validity of theories is tested by comparing one group using the theory to another group not using the theory. For example, when testing a new drug, the effectiveness and validity of the drug used by one group of testers is compared to the "control" group— that is, the sample given the "placebo." In trauma debriefing, however, it is extremely difficult to conduct research on a "control" group, victims of a tragedy who have not received any kind of formal psychological debriefing. This makes the theory of debriefing seem unsound, and therefore opens it to criticism. In fact, it has even been suggested that people who experience trauma debriefing can end up feeling worse than they did before! This controversy will probably continue for a long time. One thing is certain, though—and I am sure most readers will agree on this—when a person who has experienced a violent tragedy is able to talk about the event in a cathartic way, the possibility of repression diminishes, and recovery is more likely. Talking is good.

Naturally, I speak from a biased point of view about the trauma response. But I can see why some individuals might have misgivings or skepticism about the process. I fail, however, to see how, after a couple of hundred years of good scientific psychology starting way before Freud, anyone could suggest that families can always cope with tragedy on their own. That belittles all the advances in psychology that have been made during this century—it's like telling people to throw out their computers and go back to quill and ink.

Following a violent event in the workplace, any employer that wants to be taken seriously as caring and fair should make sure good trauma response services are available to staff. Most EAP providers throughout North America, and indeed throughout the world, have well-established trauma response services. And the price to pay for a reactive response service is small compared to the price to the employer of worker illness and disability that can be among the long-term effects of untreated trauma. Aside from EAP companies, there are networks of therapists and community critical incident response teams in many areas of Canada and the U.S. The most important concern for managers, supervisors and workplace colleagues is not to underestimate the traumatic impact of rage and violence that can be experienced at work.

Chapter 11

Rage
and Liability

The subject of employer liability, individual liability and vicarious liability is extremely tricky. I have never studied law, with the exception of the Canon Law of the Catholic Church, but a book on work rage must discuss some of the types of legislation that exist to protect employees from the effects of rage at work.

As a scare tactic, I often tell employers that they are responsible for the violent and aggressive behavior of employees, both on and off the premises . . . even all the way to the pub! My intention is to get the employer to seriously consider putting in place proper policies and procedures for the protection of employees in their care.

Here are a few pieces of legislation that are important to consider:

Legislation Regarding Canadian Human Rights
There are two sources of legislation regarding human rights in Canada. One is federal, covering all federal

government employees, chartered banks and inter-provincial institutions as contained in the *Canadian Human Rights Act*. The other source is provincial; each province has human rights legislation to protect employees in the provincial domain. Human rights legislation generally exists to protect people from discrimination and harassment on 11 prohibited grounds. These grounds are the following:

- Race
- National or ethnic origin
- Color
- Sex, including pregnancy and childbirth
- Age
- Marital status
- Religion
- Sexual orientation
- Family status
- Pardoned conviction and disability

Discrimination means acting for or against someone on the basis of preconceived bias or prejudice. *Harassment* is the unsolicited, unwanted attention that causes deliberate offence, humiliation and embarrassment. It could be argued that a racially motivated act of violence—say, a physical assault—as well as being criminally wrong, is an act of harassment. An employer would have to be careful to ensure that protective policies and procedures are in place if she or he wanted to avoid the costs associated with successful complaints under human rights legislation. Even in situations where employees themselves are violating the organization's policies and procedures, there is still an element of liability on the part of the employer following an act of workplace violence: the human rights commission might still rule that the employer violated a victim's human rights. And such commissions can make judgments for punitive damages that are costly to the organization, as well as forcing it to provide educational training and to develop better protective policies.

One important aspect of human rights legislation is that it covers areas beyond the physical, providing for such violations as mental distress and psychological pressure.

Legislation Regarding Health and Safety

For a number of years, the provinces of British Columbia and Saskatchewan have had specific health and safety legislation requiring employers to minimize the risk of injury to employees from violence in the workplace. Some of the other provinces are now tabling legislation initiatives to tackle the problem. In British Columbia, where legislation was first enacted in 1993, the statutes include the following summarized items:

1. Risk assessments must be performed in any workplace in which a risk of injury from violence may be present.

2. Where there is an assessed risk, the employer is duty-bound to create policies and procedures, and work environment arrangements to eliminate the risks of violence to employees.

3. In situations where elimination of the risk is not possible, then the employer must do what they can in terms of policy, procedure and work arrangement to minimize the risks.

4. The employer must inform the employee of the extent and nature of the risk. This duty also includes informing staff of persons (fellow employees) known to have a history of violent behavior that they may encounter at work.

5. As well as all of the above, the employer is duty-bound to educate employees on policy, procedure, reporting methods, appropriate response to violence and how to obtain assistance.

6. The employer must also make provision for post-trauma psychological support for employee victims and witnesses to violence at work.

Note that this legislation was introduced to provide an additional safety feature for employees at risk of violence from influences external to the workforce. It does not necessarily protect employees from violence perpetrated by a co-worker. However, there is also legislation in B.C. that addresses violence between co-workers (*Industrial Health and Safety Regulation*). This is all fairly comprehensive legislation, and puts the onus clearly on the employer to create and establish a safe environment even when there is an assessed risk of a potential for injury as the result of violence. In terms of liability, therefore, when an employer is not fulfilling the statutory obligations imposed in law, he or she is open to hostile litigation from various fronts, including the employee victim of violence and perhaps even employees' designated beneficiaries.

There are other provisions in law for the protection of employees from workplace violence, such as workers' compensation regulations, but given that all the provinces have different provisions, I do not intend to look at them in depth. Suffice to say that the rules of the Workers' Compensation Board (Workplace Safety and Insurance Board, in Ontario) allow for compensation to employees who are injured as a result of physical violence perpetrated by a colleague or superior at work. As well, there is the employer's potential for civil liability toward the victim, and even, sometimes, toward the perpetrator. Since these are complex areas, however, I will address only two of the more common issues arising from them.

- The victim of violence at work may believe that the conditions of the employment contract have altered as a result of his being exposed to a violent situation, and may therefore claim constructive dismissal. The victim then may take civil action against the employer for compensation in lieu of notice. Moreover, victims

136

of violence at work can also make civil claims against the employer for punitive damages.

- The employer may feel it necessary to take action against the perpetrator of violence in the workplace in order to make that workplace as safe as possible and provide protection to all other employees. But in order to win in a "termination with just cause" action, the employer has to be extremely well prepared and have documentation showing the case history and all the factors taken into consideration in the decision to terminate.

Liability is not my area of expertise, and I know I have not done justice to such an important topic. I am a great believer in consulting the experts, however, and that is what I encourage you, the reader, to do. Whether you are a leader of an organization concerned over the scope of employer liability, or an employee looking for advice, get the facts from the experts, and do not depend on the backroom lawyers!

Chapter 12

The Face
of Rage:
A Case Study

James's Story

James was a self-mutilator. And his was one of the most soul-destroying cases of rage in the workplace I ever encountered. When I first met James in counseling, he was in a state of deep crisis. He had been on the verge of severing his foot off with a powerful industrial-size lawn mower. Even an experienced counselor has a problem listening empathetically to that kind of disclosure. But that was how therapy began for James. He had stopped himself in time, and had called our employee assistance center right away, requesting help.

During the first session, James slowly and without sparing the details unfolded a story of violence in the workplace that had endured for about four years. It was his own story, of course, but at the same time it was a story of a type of systemic violence that existed within the department where he worked. He perceived that the system was treating him violently by not addressing

138

adequately the harassment he was receiving from his boss, and the only way he could take revenge on the system, in his eyes, was to injure himself. In doing so at work, he could then avoid contact with his boss by spending time both in hospital and at home recovering from the self-inflicted injuries. By the end of the first session, I had managed to get James to agree to a contract, that as long as he was attending therapy, he would not self-mutilate. This contract lasted more than two years.

My initial assessment of James was that he was badly in need of a psychiatric referral. His presenting problem for EAP counseling was beyond the normal parameters of short-term, solution-focused therapy. It seemed more likely to me that he would benefit from long-term therapy, and perhaps even a combination approach of psychotherapy and pharmacology. But James declined. He felt comfortable with me and did not want to go to anyone else. Fortunately, at that point I was being supported in my approach both by my immediate boss and by our clinical supervisor, a wonderful psychodynamic psychotherapist, whom we met with every two weeks. James's case was regularly monitored.

During those initial sessions, I tried as best I could to uncover the life history of my client. As well as finding out about all the "accidents" that were happening at work, I discovered a person whose life had been fragmented almost from day one. From an early age, he was raised in a group home with his older brother. Their parents had separated and eventually divorced, and the father was awarded custody of the two boys. It soon became clear to the father that he could not cope with the child rearing and so the decision was made to put the boys into a foster home run by a Christian organization.

Ten years passed—years when there was little contact from either the father or the mother. Yes, there were the Christmas visits or birthday treats, but no regular family life for the two boys. On reaching his 16th birthday, the older brother was released from the foster home, sent out to find his own way in the world. He joined the army and settled into that disciplined way of life, opting for the institutional lifestyle. James was alone, bereft of family contact until he reached 16 two years later.

James struggled with himself and the world for the next couple of years, until he was about 18 and his father managed to secure an interview for James with the Parks and Recreation Department where the father was employed. James then began his career as a gardener. When he started coming to counseling, he was about to become a father for the second time. He was involved in a common-law relationship with a woman about 10 or 12 years his senior, had never had a good relationship with her, but somehow clung to his family as a precious possession, despite the fact that his "partner" seemed to want little to do with him.

His work life had began to sour four years earlier, when he was transferred to another part of the city and under the supervision of a man to whom he took an instant dislike—and the feeling was mutual. Put the two of them together, and there were fireworks. The supervisor had a foul temper, shouted a lot at his staff, abused and berated them in front of each other and in public view. The department heads seemed to condone this type of behavior; when James approached his superiors, he was more or less told to shape up or ship out. He was definitely not given a sympathetic ear.

So after a couple of years of this constant hostility, he'd had enough. He decided to take action, but his thinking patterns were not the logical ones most of us would expect. Thus, the self-mutilation started: he broke his own index finger. This injury allowed him a few weeks at home, and, therefore, freedom from contact with and abuse from his boss. What a relief for him! But the relief was short-lived and the return to work painful. Within a short period, he had given himself a large cut on the thigh, followed by broken toes, a stab in the arm, another broken finger, an injured back and shoulder, a gash on the head . . . the list was endless. Management simply thought James accident-prone! By the time he met me, things had become so bad and the atmosphere had become so poisoned for him that he was ready to do himself permanent injury.

Only once do I remember James coming close to breaking his contract of non-mutilation, and that was about a year into our counselor-client relationship. I was wakened in the night by telephone. James said he was feeling like jumping in front of a bus, and it was the first time he had experienced any desire to inflict this much damage. Of course, being the supportive counselor, I wanted to get back to sleep, but decided instead to go and pick him up and take him to an emergency room for immediate support. When I found him at the other side of the city, he was in a very distressed state, and became more distressed and agitated when I suggested a visit to the hospital. Naturally, hospital was the last thing he wanted or needed. He just wanted to find a place to stay for the rest of the night since he felt he could not go home. He came home to my place, and I made him up a bed on the living room sofa. I returned to my own bed and began to worry seriously about having a potential psychopath asleep in my home. Not a good move for a therapist! And needless to say, I did not sleep much for the rest of the night.

James had a lot going on inside his head. His problems were rooted in the insecurities he had felt all through his life, and there was probably some residual trauma from his childhood playing out in his relationship with his supervisor. His thinking pattern, or cognitive functioning, was emotionally based on what he saw as his "ideal." He did not want to end his life, because he could not imagine his own daughter and son being without the love and care of a father. He was a proud parent, and a loving one. In fact, nothing gave him more pleasure than being at home, looking after the children. But he also wanted to provide for them the best way he could.

As a therapist, I was dealing with many layers of

complexity in James's story. One of the main issues for me was the fact that James had confessed himself to be at risk, and it was, therefore, my duty to find ways to protect him. Contracting with him to stop the self-mutilating was a first step, but because of the danger he posed to himself, he also posed a danger to the supervisor, to his colleagues and to the public. A second issue was that I became obligated to inform his department, and in particular those responsible for human resources, in order to establish protective measures. Following are a few of the other considerations in this complex case:

- James's history was one of deep insecurity and emotional instability. If you look at the profile of the potential violent offender (Chapter 2), James fits almost perfectly, although his violence was directed toward himself.
- The work environment, the system, promoted an atmosphere of disrespect, hostility, conflict and distrust.
- There were concerns on my part around liability, both of the manager and the department, but no one seemed interested in this aspect of the problem. What if James were to take revenge on someone other than himself? What would the legal consequences be for the leadership of the department?
- Leadership seemed uninterested in finding a workable solution. They wanted to abrogate their responsibilities.

- The supervisor was defended on the basis that he was good at his job. However, no leadership training had ever been offered to him, and the department had no method in place for evaluating the effectiveness of his leadership. Therefore, each leader became a law unto himself. The department would always defend a leader before listening to the concerns of an employee considered to be dispensable.

- Human Resources, instead of advocating on behalf of the employees and their concerns, became the policing authority for sickness and absenteeism.

- Other employees in similar situations with this supervisor just had to grin and bear it. No one wanted to listen.

- Although there was anti-harassment policy and procedure, it was not taken seriously.

In hindsight, I often imagine a better outcome and solution than the one eventually agreed upon for James. After using up all his accrued sick time, about a full year, he was persuaded to accept retirement on the grounds of ill health. This solution allowed him to spend time at home, while receiving a small pension. But it did mean that our therapeutic relationship had to terminate. At that point, he felt ready to take a referral, and since I had already planned for this ahead of time, I had a good psychiatrist waiting in the wings—one who was an expert assessing the origins of, and treating, self-mutilation. From time to time James popped in to our counseling center to say hi.

He was slowly taking time to rediscover his attachments and connection to his family, in particular his brother and father. However, he remained a man pained with his life experience.

Observations

Based on my handling of this and similar cases, both here in Canada and in Scotland, I can make a few observations about James's story and recommendations for organizations that really want to make a difference in how they promote a safe working environment.

Observation 1: Disappointment

James felt let down. His parents had disappointed him by divorcing and farming him off to a foster home. Society had let him down, too, by making him spend his growing years in an institution that religiously regimented his upbringing and then dumped him on the street at age 16, unprepared for life alone. To add fuel to the fire, his workplace disappointed him greatly. He was a hard worker, showed respect to his colleagues and bosses, and wanted only a fair day's pay for a fair day's work. But he got abused and harassed, and no one would listen, take it seriously or show any concern. He was disrespected. He felt violated.

Life was adding up to one big disappointment, and so he decided to take matters into his own hands. If he hurt himself, he would hurt the system, because the system would have to pay.

Observation 2: The Workplace Can Make a Difference

There is nothing a workplace can do to address the disappointments in the life of someone like James. The workplace does not exist to cure the staff's preexisting turmoil. It can, however, address carefully the disappointment that staff experience when the workplace lets them down. The workplace leadership can deploy fair methods to address systemic abuse by introducing reliable and realistic procedures for reporting and investigating incidents of workplace violence. As has been indicated elsewhere in this book, such procedures need the blessing of the entire leadership, beginning at the top, and they need to be seen to be practiced at all levels within the organization.

Recommendations

If I were to be faced with a "James" today, I admit that I would change my approach.

- *Use the experts.* There is expert advice available from qualified psychiatrists on the strangest and most unlikely mental illnesses. I would insist more assertively that the client undergo a *professional psychiatric assessment*, emphasizing the organizational concern around the client's potential for physical harm to the self or to others. As an outside consultant to organizations today, I often make this recommendation to use the experts. They may not get it right every single time, but it is well worth the effort and expense in the long term if the organization really wants to protect staff and make them feel safe at work.

- *Communicate with the top of the organization.* In James's case, people at the lower levels in the hierarchy were all floundering around, avoiding any decision-making. When there is a danger to the organization, or to individuals, the person who should take decisive action is the one for whom the liability issues are clear: the person at the top. It often happens, though, that the one at the top is unreachable or unapproachable. In this scenario, I would recommend going to the person known to have the most influence and to be the most reasonable.

- *Offer more proactive consultation to the organization.* I would offer more assistance to the organization around their systemic issues, and collaborate with them to take a positive stand to eradicate outdated and inappropriate managerial styles. Ten or twelve years ago, I was probably perceived as immature and lacking the wherewithal to offer advice on these issues. Now, more experience, a bit thicker around the waist and with a few gray hairs around the temple, I probably would be taken more seriously. The point is this: an organization needs to consult with people who have knowledge about workplace violence. Rage and violence may not be areas of interest for most people, but there does exist in North America a great deal of expertise around a) the promotion of safe environments and b) methods for the eradication of violence at work. Many organizations would think nothing of using expert consulting services for their computer systems or for their restructuring program. But how many would be willing to invest money to make the workplace free from rage? A growing number, I hope.

Conclusion

Most organizations have a James . . . or a Tom . . . or a Sarah or whoever. And many of them would never recognize that the James/Tom/Sarah issues derive from an organizational issue. Many would be willing to run the risk of doing nothing to address the problem of rage at work, whatever its guise. In James's case, the rage turned inward; and he vented it at himself in such a way that the organization might never have been aware of the problem. And rage can show up in many different disguises. The organization has to keep eyes, ears, indeed all the senses open in order to know what is going on. Preventing workplace violence is far less costly than fixing the damage that can otherwise result.

Postscript

For interested readers, James' actual diagnosis by me and by the psychiatrist who treated him after me was borderline personality disorder.

Chapter 13

Respect in the Workplace

Often opportunities come my way to seek out other people's opinions about a multitude of workplace issues. One of the most rewarding has been the solicitation of workers' opinions on the topic of respect in the workplace. The number of ideas and creative responses that this type of opinion-seeking generates is incredible. For example, in one workshop, I asked the question, *What do you think contributes to respect at work?* The replies included the following:

- Accepting
- Tolerating
- Being willing to be open
- Saying "hello" and "goodbye"
- Thanking
- Praising
- Expecting from others what you would do for them
- Giving fair treatment

- Collaborating
- Upholding equality
- Not talking back to someone
- Giving people their personal space
- Listening when someone is speaking to you
- Maintaining eye contact, if culturally appropriate
- Not saying anything unless it is nice
- Understanding that "No" means "No"
- Being able to delegate

When all the attributes are added up, that one little word *respect* takes on wide-ranging significance. Of course, we saw in Chapter 11 that human rights legislation exists federally and provincially to protect employees' rights to respect and dignity in the workplace. However, just because legislation exists does not guarantee that people will be respected and their dignity upheld! It has been my experience that when there is lack of respect shown toward employees, the potential for aggressive behavior increases. When people are not shown respect, stress levels rise. When stress levels rise, the danger of rage also rises.

Respect, and consequently trust, in the workplace disappears when attitudes of superiority creep in and infect the environment. And these attitudes sometimes appear almost by accident. Imagine a hypothetical situation in which a large part of a huge organization is sold off to be run as an independent business unit. There follows a period of downsizing. Many of the employees have been long-term employees of the former parent company, and take the generous severance packages offered. The remaining staff—mainly a White, Anglo-Saxon group—because of their seniority, work hard on the day shift, and life goes on with some semblance of normalcy. Business improves, and staff are required. The organization recruits for a night shift and hires a large group of multiethnic employees, retained on a minimum-wage basis, earning half as much as their counterparts with wage guarantees on the day shift. Problems arise. Communication between the two shifts is fractured, to say the least. Small incidents of inter-shift conflict grow, culminating in racial slurs, taunts regarding sexual orientation, sexist comments directed to women.

What do you think happens to common respect? Well, it is long gone by the time rage blows out of control and drives one employee to throw a metal crowbar at another.

In this scenario, many of the attributes of respect were missing from the start: equality, tolerance, acceptance, fair treatment, thanks, praise. And because this hypothetical organization was newly formed, it had not yet found the means within policies and procedures to establish equitable practices and introduce measures for the smooth integration of new employees into the existing workforce.

People often tell me they believe that respect has to be earned; that it is not automatically granted. Meanwhile, I try to foster a more reasonable approach that says respect is automatic for every human being because we recognize diversity and individuality. Many argue with me that if a person does not *show* respect, the person is not *worthy* of respect. That, too, is reasonable to suggest. If I take that stance, however, I am beginning to perpetuate the disrespect. And that becomes counterproductive to the idea of accepting diversity and individuality.

On the contrary, the notion of respect, especially in the workplace, has to begin with the common ground of unconditional acceptance of the other as a warm-blooded, sentient human being. But this can be a tough belief to put into practice.

Work rage might gradually disappear, I like to think, if the belief that all people are worthy of respect were accepted and put into practice in today's workplace.

Chapter 14
Rage and Risk Assessment

Part I: The Crisis Management Team

Every organization that intends to take seriously the problem of rage in the workplace must be prepared for the eventuality of violent behavior by having a workplace anti-violence program in effect. This is the only way to really tackle the problem. Leaving it to good luck or chance is not enough, and you never know when your luck is going to run out. In order to get a program started, the organization must look at the problem systematically and systemically. This requires introspection on the part of a team—whose role is identified by the name Crisis Management Team, or something similar—of competent and interested representatives from various levels of responsibility within the organization.

How big should the team be and who should be part of it? The size of the crisis management team will depend on the size of the organization. For small companies of fewer than 50 employees, a few members may be enough. For larger organizations representing a couple of thousand employees, an efficient team size would be 10 to 15 people, with enough representation to carry out all the necessary functions.

Senior Management

A crisis management team cannot operate well without at least minimal representation from senior management, and, at a very minimum, from the vice presidential level. This presence from the upper echelons sends a message to staff that the team is worthy, and that its business is serious and encourages cooperation. It is also useful to have a senior representative since someone, at some time, is going to have to make decisions that affect many employees. If this senior person is seen to have defined authority as opposed to delegated authority, it's easier for everyone else on the team. By defined authority I mean that the person has the ability to make decisions without reference to a superior within the organization, and by delegated authority I refer to the person who always has to refer decision-making to the person for whom she or he is delegate. It is much easier for someone on the team to have the ability to make decisions quickly and authoritatively.

Unions

If your organization has a labor union, then this is one time when all of you can work together for the safety of the entire workforce. Differences can be, and must be, set aside in order for the crisis management team to be effective. It has been my privilege to work closely with the union leaders and stewards in a number of organizations when the crisis management teams have been initiated. When there is close collaboration and a putting aside of adversarial relationships, the organization has greater success in meeting the team's goals. In a unionized environment, the best advocate for introducing anti-violence policies and procedures is the union itself.

Human Resources

The policy makers within organizations tend to be found in human resources departments. The whole *raison d'être* for HR lies in the department's ability to set quantifiable standards for hiring, firing, retention, benefits and a host of other issues. Their role in a crisis management team is vital, particularly for the design, development and delivery of a *zero tolerance policy* that reflects the cultural norms of the organization they represent. In the unlikely event of a death resulting from violence at work, it is also useful for the HR professional to act as liaison between the organization and the family of the deceased.

Security

Most organizations nowadays have a security division—people whose expertise can be highly valuable on a crisis management team. Security tends to know areas of difficulty and have a sense of who will be a problem within an organization. From both the practical and the legal point of view, the inclusion of security in an anti-violence campaign or program is vital. Trained security staff will display appropriate intervention skills. You can't underestimate the value they bring to an organization.

Legal Counsel

If the organization is lucky enough to have its own full-time legal advisor or department, then full use of the skills and expertise around areas of corporate, individual and vicarious liability should be brought to the crisis management team. If your organization does not have in-house legal counsel, try to make sure that you obtain the best possible advice by consulting over liability issues with the organization's designated corporate lawyer.

Public Relations

Should your organization be faced with a tragic violent incident, you have to be prepared to communicate the event in the best possible way to employees, families and the public. Professionals in public relations bring to the crisis management team the wisdom of good communication skills, and sometimes the "spin" techniques that are often necessary in the aftermath of disaster. It is often an advantage for the public relations representatives to be involved in the crisis management team from the outset, since their familiarity with existing protocols and procedures in the organization means that they are prepared for "surprises."

Risk Management

The risk management function within an organization, simply put, brings to the team another area of expertise: risk assessment. Although their expertise may not be specifically in the area of vulnerability for violence, they will still bring methodology and technique to the crisis management process.

Occupational Health and Safety

For occupational health and safety experts, the well-being of all staff is a primary concern, be it in terms of keeping the workforce healthy or creating a safe environment. It's necessary to include them on the team, since these professionals in the field of safety or nursing are sometimes the first in the organization to know when there is a potential danger in the workplace from an employee. There is more likely to be employee "trust" in occupational health representatives than in human resources representatives, given that HR is often thought of as the "terminator," a term that in itself has a violent connotation.

Part II: Functions of the Crisis Management Team

To pull a team together, members must have a defined purpose in the life of the organization. And that purpose, as I see it, is to diminish the potential for violence and generally make "work" a better place to be. If the first step is to bring together representatives from all the varied organizational functions, the second is to assign functions to those representatives. The team should meet regularly at first, and then at frequent intervals, once the responsibilities are being carried out on an ongoing basis or have been completed satisfactorily.

The functions of the team include the following:

- Risk assessment
- Policy development
- Prevention programs
- Orientation for new employees
- Crisis response and investigation
- Trauma response services organization
- Communication with senior management

Risk Assessment

The team's first function is to undertake an assessment of the organization's risk for violence. Some call this risk assessment a "violence vulnerability audit" or a "threat inventory." Whatever the label, the purpose is the same: to examine the organization carefully to recognize and understand the potential for violent incidents. The results of the risk assessment should indicate to the organization the need for further work, such as setting up prevention programs, creating policies and procedures, implementing education and training programs or taking crisis response measures.

The following items should be included in the risk assessment tool.

Risk History

- Incidents of violent behavior within the past year

_____

_____

- How severe were the incidents?

_____

- How many were there?

_____

- Where did they occur?

_____

- How many people did they involve?

_____

- What actually happened?

_____

_____

- Was the incident perpetrated by a) outsider/stranger,
  b) co-worker, c) family member/relative/friend, d)
  manager/supervisor?

_____

- At what time of day did it occur?

_____

- In which area of our business?

_____

- What types of job classification were the victims? a)
  managers, b) supervisors, c) front-line staff/customer
  service, d) janitorial, e) security

_____

_____

_____

Work Environment

- How many locations (branches) are there?

  _____

- Is the location known to be in a violent neighbor-hood?

  _____

- How many staff work in each location?

  _____

- What kind of floor plan is in each environment?

  _____

- How many unsecured entrances and exits are there?

  _____

- What type of perimeter lighting is installed?

  _____

- Is there security, staff, alarms, a buddy system?

  _____

- What kind of shift patterns do we observe?

  _____

  _____

- What are the hours of operation? Do we operate weekends? (High-risk time is 9 p.m. to 6 a.m.)

  _____

  _____

  _____

Staffing and Policy

- What is the age range of staff?

  _____

- What is the breakdown in gender (males/females)?

  _____

  _____

- What kind of appearance do we promote (casual/formal/professional?)

  _____

  _____

- Do we have a multiracial and multicultural work-force?

  _____

  _____

- What kind of employee personalities do we attract as an employer?

  _____

  _____

- What kind of attitudes do we encourage?

  _____

  _____

- Is there an atmosphere where everyone feels respected?

  _____

  _____

- Is our compensation package considered satisfactory?

  _____

  _____

- What kind of health promotion benefits do we offer?

  _____

  _____

- What benefits do we offer for short- and long-term disability?

  _____

  _____

- Do we have a generally healthy workforce?

  _____

  _____

- What levels of stress are currently being experienced by staff?

  _____

  _____

- Are we considered to handle terminations fairly?

  _____

  _____

- Do we have rehabilitation programs (for alcohol addiction/drug addiction/relapse prevention after treatment)?

  _____

  _____

- Do we have a good human rights history?

  _____

  _____

- Do we have policies and procedures for the following?
  a) Maternity leave

  _____

  b) Discrimination and harassment

  _____

  c) Code of conduct on behavior at work

  _____

d) Business code of conduct

_____

e) Zero tolerance of violence

_____

- Are we perceived to be a "caring" employer?

_____

_____

Contact with the Public

- Do any of our business operations involve exchange of money?

_____

_____

- Where do we locate our cash registers?

_____

_____

- Do we sell/deliver/dispense drugs/alcohol/tobacco?

_____

_____

- Do we have face-to-face customer service operations?

_____

_____

- Do we have telephone customer service?

_____

_____

- Would any of our staff expect to be abused by the public
  a) Physically, e.g., pushing and pulling?

  _____

  b) Verbally, e.g., yelling and screaming?

  _____

  c) Emotionally, e.g., threatening, making racial slurs?

  _____

- Are we involved in providing health care?

  _____

- Do we deal with psychiatric patients?

  _____

- Do we handle potentially violent criminals?

  _____

- Is abuse considered a necessary evil, a part of the job?

  _____

- Do we have a unionized environment?

  _____

- Do we have a record of adversarial relationships?

  _____

- Do we settle disputes quickly?

  _____

- Have there ever been lingering effects of a strike?

  _____

- Do we keep emergency services numbers handy?

  _____

The above only scratches the surface. A risk assessment tool has to be comprehensive. It's an organization's reality check. Each group then has to look more closely at each of the areas to identify substrata and discover trends. But that, really, is the beauty of developing a team approach. The responsibility does not become a burden on one person; instead, it relies on the expertise of many. Remember, the risk assessment is going to be your measuring stick to determine your further needs and requirements as you tackle the problem of workplace rage. From there will evolve the organization's program of prevention and education.

Policy Development
Another function of the crisis management team is to be proactive in creating a workplace policy, and accompanying set of procedures, on zero tolerance of violence. The policy should be as clear as possible in six main areas:

- Purpose of the policy
- Definition of violence in the workplace
- Declaration of responsibility for the entire workforce
- General outline of sanctions for policy breaches
- Confidential reporting mechanisms and documentation
- Action to be taken by victims and witnesses

Purpose of the Policy

Any policy development is usually governed by its purpose. And a "zero tolerance of violence" policy has to state clearly that the organization really wants to do everything in its power to create an environment free from the potential harm of violent behavior, and safe for employees, visitors, guests and contractors. The purpose statement, therefore, has to indicate the *commitment* from the top of the organization to eradicate any form of abusive or violent conduct at work.

Definition of Violence in the Workplace

In order that there be no room for misinterpretation, the policy should also indicate exactly what behavior the organization considers "violent." I find it best if organizations do not limit their definition to a general statement about aggressive or intimidating behavior. Rather, the definition should state in clear and precise terms what is meant by violent behavior—physical, verbal, emotional *and* psychological. In Chapter 1, you will recall, I defined violence in the following way:

> Workplace rage is any physical assault, behavior considered to be threatening or abuse in a verbal manner that occurs in the work setting. It has to include, but is not limited to the following examples: beatings, stabbing, suicides and near-suicides, rapes and shootings. Rage also includes inducing psychological trauma through such

means as obscene phone calls, threats and a presence of another person that can be considered intimidating. As well as this, the definition of rage should include any type of harassment, such as being sworn at, shouted at or stalked.

Any policy has to be this specific, and also must list examples. I know that many policy makers like to keep policy documents general, and define the details later. I think this is the wrong approach. When we are dealing with rage and violent behavior, the policy document itself has to specify *all* unacceptable behavior.

Declaration of Responsibility

The responsibility for creating a workplace that is free from the effects of violent behavior must be shared by all staff. This has to include management, of course, but it is not the sole responsibility of the executives at the top to create a safe environment. Every individual in the organization must be reminded that it is the personal duty of all to help in the eradication of abuse. And whenever applicable, a policy should also note that the labor union has a part to play in developing an anti-violence strategy.

Sanctions

The policy must indicate that threats of any intent to harm and all other infringements of the policy will be taken seriously. And the organization must be willing to adhere to its policy, show its commitment to the anti-violence strategy and impose sanctions when breaches are reported. Sanctions can be outlined in a general way, but have to ensure that the punishment fits the crime. For example, to transfer a long-term employee with an otherwise clean record simply for using abusive language would be excessive. In such a case, perhaps a simple apology would suffice. The policy should give examples of sanctions, and should always include the "up to and including termination" phrase. It is also helpful to state the fact that in some instances, violators may be subject not only to sanctions, but to criminal prosecution.

Reporting and Documentation

Staff within organizations need to be encouraged to report their experiences of intimidation and violence. This should be outlined in the policy, but, in addition, the organization needs to create a system by which employees can "safely" report incidents without fear of recrimination. It is easy to state in a policy "All staff should report threats of any kind to their manager, supervisor or HR representative," but employees may not find the process easy to follow, especially in cases involving intimidation from a manager. The crisis management team should be assigned the task of hearing and investigating the employee reports, and the policy should designate it as such. This process should not be seen to replace the normal rights to grievance that a unionized employee may already have. Neither should it be seen to replace a manager's or supervisor's normal tasks of monitoring employee performance and behavior.

Designating the team as the reporting authority within the organization also makes it easier to track documentation, such as numbers of reports and outcomes of investigations. Crisis management team members bring a level of objectivity and impartiality to the investigation process, and add credibility to the organization's commitment to prevent violence.

Action by Victims and Witnesses

When a process earns credibility in the workplace, more people will be willing to use it to address their issues. If the crisis management team is seen to be effective, people who are victimized at work or who witness any kind of victimization will feel more empowered to take action. The policy, therefore, has to make it clear that employees, regardless of their position within the organization, and regardless of any relationship they may have to the instigator or the victim of violence, have a duty to report. This action is an affirmative step in supporting the philosophical basis of zero tolerance.

Prevention Programs

Although all the above-mentioned functions of the crisis management team involve violence prevention in the workplace, other specific tasks can add to the organization's commitment to anti-violence. These tasks relate to the design of an educational program that will heighten anti-violence awareness among employees. The team should adopt responsibility for the design and content of managerial and supervisory training programs in such areas as how to deal with emotionally charged situations, as well as developing the necessary short educational programs necessary to familiarize staff with zero-tolerance policy and procedures. Note that although the team members might not necessarily be the right people to deliver the training and education, it is important that the team bring to any prevention program the concerns raised during the risk assessment, ensuring that areas of weakness within the organization are addressed.

Prevention programs can also be enhanced through consultation with professionals, institutions and agencies that have a vested interest in anti-violence at work. Liaison with the local police department, security experts, employee assistance or crisis response experts might prove useful.

Orientation for New Employees

From day one, a new employee should be introduced to members of the crisis management team and given an "anti-violence orientation." This sets a high standard, and gets the new employee off on the right foot, signaling that the company takes workplace safety seriously enough to put it ahead of everything else. The orientation should include the following:

- Delivery of the policy and procedures
- Explanation of how the policy and sanctions work
- Demonstration of security measures and why they exist
- Names, photographs and contact numbers of the risk management team
- Methods for staying safe—for example, a buddy system

Crisis Response and Investigation

The crisis management team should be on call to respond to incidents of violence as they happen. Just as hospitals have a variety of crisis response codes, so, too, should organizations develop a series of codes that will alert the team of an incident of threatened or actual violence, and of their need to attend.

Normally, by the time the team arrives at the scene, a couple of things have already happened: a) the incident is over and b) there is chaos. The crisis management team swings into action to take control of the chaos and start the investigation. Quick assessment is necessary: Is there a need for first aid? the police? death notification? family liaison? nourishment and water? trauma response counseling? Depending on the circumstances, it may be only necessary to have a few members of the crisis management team at the scene. Other members of the team, at a designated control center, might accomplish some of the more pressing tasks.

When it comes to post-incident investigation, there are a number of tasks to accomplish—and quickly.

- Visit the scene of the incident quickly to find out the exact circumstances and to build up a physical picture of what happened.
- Initiate the process of interviewing anyone who was injured, threatened or intimidated, including victims and witnesses. Do this with tact and diplomacy. Remember that the victims and the witnesses may be suffering the effects of traumatic stress.
- Uncover any reports of prior inappropriate behavior, if the perpetrator was an employee. If the incident was perpetrated from outside, ask about security measures, forced entry and employee preparedness and training for hostile behavior. For example, in robbery situations, have staff been trained in robbery protocol and trauma?
- In organizational debriefing, determine reasons for the incident, how it could have been prevented and any measures needed to make the environment safer.
- Record and document all the investigation findings in a central location, including different types of intervention required in the aftermath of the incident, for example, medical treatment, trauma interventions, enhanced security measures and standby staffing support.

Trauma Response Services

It is the responsibility of the crisis management team, I would suggest, to be a liaison with other company stakeholders in retaining a trauma response provider adequate to the needs of the organization. Other stakeholders in this instance would be the members of the employee assistance program committee, the unions and human resources and finance departments staff. In your selection process, look for the following attributes:

- Can your trauma response service respond around the clock, seven days a week? Sometimes intervention may not be required immediately, but it can be useful to have an immediate professional assessment.

- Will the service guarantee professional therapists, trained to deal specifically with trauma and critical incidents? It is becoming more common to find well-intentioned and highly experienced volunteers from the community as members of crisis response teams. But in today's world of legislation and vicarious liability, it is wise to question your provider's cover for liability, especially if there is protective legislation in your province.

- Will the provider be able to make appropriate referrals to an EAP, to community resources or to private therapists for the continuation of treatment, if required? Given what we discussed earlier in terms of trauma debriefing and its effectiveness, it is good practice to have a backup plan in place for people suffering lingering effects of exposure to aggression and violence. Make sure your provider can assist with this.

- Choose a provider that best fits your needs in terms of image, industry experience, size, availability (locally and nationally) and proven expertise. Keep in mind that having an understanding of your own corporate culture, management style and practice will help your trauma response provider do a better job.

Communication with Senior Management

It is vital that senior management be informed of all violent incidents that occur in the workplace. I mention this for one reason. Most people in business try to make a profit from their operations for the shareholders. Violence is bad news for business. Rage in the workplace, whether it starts inside or is perpetrated from outside, has an adverse effect on operations. After a violent episode, productivity drops, morale diminishes, stress levels rise—and this can have a ripple effect on the share price quoted in the stock markets.

There are also a growing number of ethical investors who are weeding out from their portfolios companies with a history of negligent attitudes toward and treatment of employees. Companies with a bad track record on conditions of employment, compensation and safety are at risk. This is certainly true for organizations that use "slave labor" to produce inexpensively the products they sell and distribute at highly inflated prices.

However, it might also apply to businesses that have experienced a violent episode that has become public knowledge. It would be interesting to investigate further the effects of violence on businesses from a point of view of lost trade, market share and market value!

As has been demonstrated, the functions of the crisis management team are varied and vital. And mostly, as suggested earlier, the very existence of such a team will depend on the organization's determination and commitment to wipe out the insidious effects of violence in the workplace. Whether yours is a large public organization or a relatively small privately owned business does not matter. The risks are the same. You cannot predict with any accuracy, if at all, when you are going to be on the receiving end of violence. The people at Xerox in Hawaii were shocked when a co-worker gunned down seven of their colleagues. The men in the Seattle shipyard did not even know the villain with the gun who killed two of them and wounded another two. I am not saying that a crisis management team will reduce to zero the potential for violence in your workplace: certain factors will always remain unpredictable. What I am saying is that there are measures you can take to reduce the probability of such episodes. By encouraging a safe environment, by making your organization zero-tolerant, and by creating policy to address all kinds of incidents, you show your commitment to respect among staff, and to the reduction of rage and violence.

Chapter 15

Rage Resolution with Employee Assistance

Since the introduction of employee assistance programs (EAPs) in Canada more than 20 years ago, the range of services available to the individual client and to the organization has increased dramatically. Mainstream counseling—that is, psychological counseling services available to individuals as part of their extended employee benefits package—will always be the cornerstone. But there are now a huge number of other services that work together toward making work a healthier, happier place to be.

I believe employee assistance companies are among the best equipped to offer services that help in establishing workplaces that are as free as possible from the effects of rage. I say this not only because I happen to be involved in the industry, but because I know from experience that the EAP family of companies possesses the skill-sets required to coordinate training and education, policies and procedures, and post-incident services such as trauma response and counseling.

Individual Employee Assistance

In a general way, employees can use the mainstream counseling service for practically anything they want: emotional problems, career counseling, stress management, dealing with a problem teenager, alcohol or substance abuse issues, sexual dysfunction, relationship breakdown. Any personal issue can find its way into a counseling office and find a supportive counselor, ready to help.

As well, most EAP providers have a series of extended services through which the caller can be connected to and receive advice from an expert in one of a variety of professions, including the following: legal, financial, child/elder care, nursing and nutrition. Over and above these extended services, EAP providers are now into the Internet, where there are chat rooms monitored by professional therapists, and bulletin boards offering advice and information on a self-help basis, as well as on-line testing and treatment for personal stress.

An EAP can offer to the individual advice on the following work rage issues:

- Managing anger
- Managing stress
- Dealing with interpersonal conflict
- Communicating assertively
- Receiving respect at work
- Saying "Stop" to the harasser
- Coping with a changing environment

- Stopping the cycle of domestic abuse
- Developing self-esteem, confidence and control

All therapists working in EAP are highly skilled at dealing with these types of scenarios. But we also have to remember that, on average, only about 7 to 10 percent of employees ever make use of an EAP service that is made available to them. So another approach to making work a better place is to have corporate drive.

Organizational Assistance Program

As the years have passed and the sophistication of EAP for the individual client has grown, so, too, have the services available to the organizational client. One of the services that evolved from a new and better understanding of client need is the trauma response service, which we have already described in detail in an earlier chapter. An EAP can act for the organizational client through its expertise in training, education and other support needed to prevent and deal with work rage.

Wellness

The large majority of EAP providers, both in the United States and in Canada, offer wellness programs. Some programs are advanced in that they offer a wide range of what might be considered "alternative " health models, such as the following:

- Massage therapy
- Aromatherapy
- Reflexology
- Acupuncture
- Naturopathic and homeopathic medicine
- Biofeedback

While some EAP providers have embraced and endorsed a large number of alternative therapies, the Canadian EAP approach to wellness is still fairly traditional and limited.

Most here offer the brown-bag seminar—that is, seminars designed to be conducted over the lunch break. The approach is basic, mainly beginner-level, and so the information provided is general in scope. But the range of topics broad, and can include some of the following:

- Balancing work and family life
- Depression—how to spot the telltale signs
- Stress management on the job
- Change management for managers
- Coping with the effects of change of work
- Problem children—how to cope
- Preparing for the later years

A number of topics from a wellness seminar list would be extremely helpful in making the workplace safer.

- Violence in the workplace—looking out for the signs

- Conflict resolution—what to do when there is conflict
- Respect—how to maintain and foster human rights at work
- Domestic violence—who to tell and what to do
- Dealing with the difficult customer or client

My own favorite topic at the moment is *respect*. However, many of the topics related to rage would, in one way or another, be appropriate for any workplace wellness approach. By providing to staff a series of workshops on topics like the ones listed above, the organization is sending a clear message of intent about the kind of environment it wants to foster.

Consulting

One of the most underestimated attributes of EAP providers is their ability and expertise as consultants. As indicated earlier, an organization would think nothing of retaining a systems expert when needing consultation around IT, but far fewer take the problem of work rage seriously enough to seek out expert opinion and advice. Consultation is an area in which the EAP companies can really prove their value to the organizational client. People who manage EAP businesses—those in sales, marketing and account management—often come from clinical backgrounds. Their grounding was in counseling, but they take that a step further by moving from the therapy side to the operations side. These individuals know the "people" world, know organizations, and can map out for the organizational client the business implications of change, stress, conflict, depression, divorce and rage in the workplace, to name but a few.

It is not my intention here to market EAPs. Rather, I would like to raise awareness of services that are underused by the thousands of organizations that currently contract with an EAP provider, in both Canada and the U.S.

In terms of preventing and dealing with work rage, EAP companies can provide consulting expertise in the following areas:

- Organizational needs assessment
- Employee attitude surveys
- Risk assessment tools
- Crisis management team building
- Robbery prevention
- Managing aggressive employees
- Managing aggressive customers
- Zero-tolerance policy development

The above is just a sampling. Of course, a national or international provider would be able to provide assistance on all these topics, while a small local EAP provider might not have the comprehensive services to do so.

Crisis Response Training

EAP providers know how to deal with a crisis. Call-center staff work day and night, constantly assessing employees and family members for the risk of suicide, homicide, abuse and more. Counseling staff know crisis work intimately, too. Therefore, it is not unusual for EAP staff to be involved in training *other* people how to behave and respond in a crisis. This is an area, I am glad to say, that employers are using more today than they were five years ago.

Within an organization, staff need to be trained in crisis response. Needless to say, it makes little sense to select a team of organizational representatives to join a risk management team or crisis intervention team without training them in the basics of crisis response. Among them are:

- Trauma response—what is a trauma?
- Physical, emotional and cognitive reactions to crisis
- Who is a victim?
- Disaster classifications, including conceptual, sensorial and duration issues
- How to begin the process of defusing a crisis
- Confronting death and dying
- How to make a death notification
- Preparation and post-incident recovery for the crisis responder

As well as theoretical training, there has to be a practical component that will clarify the various roles that members of a crisis response team will have to play in the event of an incident. This part of the training may have to be designed by the organizational client, since it deals with matters of internal structure. It should include some of the following:

- First aid
- Crowd control at the scene of an incident
- Access to the media
- Death notification
- Liaison with family members

Although at 20 years of age EAP is still considered to be a "young" business in Canada, its origins go back almost 50 or 60 years. In the United Kingdom, for example, it has been common for large organizations to offer employees "employee welfare services." The employee welfare services of such organizations as Cadbury, British Telecom and the Post Office have been around far longer than even the North American self-help groups Alcoholics Anonymous or Al-Anon. In fact, there is a professional organization in the U.K. called the Institute of Welfare Officers, with hundreds of members throughout the country. The "welfare officer" in the U.K. is the equivalent of the EAP counselor here in North America. And the institute could be compared to a professional college or association, members (officers) of which are required to meet stringent standards in education and practice, and are bound by a code of ethics.

When originally founded in North America, the main function of employee assistance was understood to be the assessment and treatment of alcohol and drug abuse addictions interfering with the individual's ability to perform well at work. EAP has come a long way since then, and will certainly continue to evolve. No longer is it a resource solely for individuals within organizations. The organization itself can be the EAP client, and can be supported and empowered by wellness, consulting and training services. As such, I believe, EAP can be an extremely valuable step on the path toward resolving rage in the workplace.

Chapter 16

Rage:
The Future
Challenge

Picture this.

- The year is 2010, and the New Millennium celebrations are but a faint memory.
- Quebec has had yet another referendum, and it remains Quebec.
- Preston Manning still leads the Opposition—always a bridesmaid, never the bride!
- The "greenback" is at par! (If only!)
- The 2008 Olympics were a great hit in Toronto, but the price is going to be paid for the next 10 years! Viva Montreal!
- Oil is scarce, again!
- There is a wee house on the moon!
- I am about to retire—very early.

Some things change; others remain the same. Technology advances, but traffic is at a standstill on major arteries. Health care is superb, but cancer rates continue to climb. The economy is growing, but downsizing still exists and is now called "resource modification." The national homicide figure continues to tumble, but rage is on the rise in the workplace. As Satchmo used to sing, "What a wonderful world!"

Back here in 2000, statistics indicate that although the national homicide rate is stable, there is an increasing problem with workplace violence. In fact, throughout North America, workplace violence is the fastest-growing category of crime. The challenge, as I see it, is to correct the current trend before the year 2010. As a society, surely we do not want to advance 10 years in technology, health care, politics, economics, housing and education, and yet still be struggling with the problem of work rage. But what is the solution?

Throughout this work, I have tried to identify some of the roots of work rage, and have indicated some of the solutions that I see as feasible. At this point, however, I have to express my own fear that all of this together will still not be enough to eradicate the problem. I firmly believe there have to be other societal approaches— approaches that take some of the burden off the employer and employee.

Family

What we do in our own homes is our own business, as long as we are acting within the confines of the law that is designed and promulgated to protect us. However, behaving one way in the home and another way at work opens up avenues for confusion. Think of a child who is expected to behave in a disciplined way at school: to sit, listen, learn and interact with other children and teachers for eight hours. What if that same child returns to a home where there is no set of rules to follow, no courtesy expected, no respect given or received? Does this not send the child mixed messages? There is a place in the family circle, I believe, for demonstrating and thus teaching the ability to control anger, resolve conflict and heal wounds.

The urge to resolve conflict by fighting and inflicting pain may arguably be a natural one, but it constitutes a negative resolution—one that is too often portrayed in media, movies and computer games. Positive resolutions of rage need to be taught. And the family, as the child's greatest influence, needs to be the teacher. Children should not be sheltered from parents' conflict resolution when it is conducted in a respectful and non-threatening way.

My argument is simple. I see parents—or whoever fulfills the parental role—as having a responsibility to model values and life skills for the younger members of the family. Among these is the ability to resolve conflict without pain and hurt.

School and Education

Recently, I learned that in the past year, the Toronto police department has confiscated more than 5,200 weapons from students in Toronto schools. I was shocked—not just by the number, but by the fact that weapons are in the schools in the first place. Why would any student wish, or feel the need, to carry a weapon?

The problem of school rage is, indeed, a serious one, and it warrants careful investigation and research. It is not just saddening but horrifying to see the results over the past few years. Littleton, Colorado, and Taber, Alberta, come to mind. In both highly reported incidents, the loss of life and injury affected a large number of families, as well as the local communities.

School boards have a tough task. They must not only try to create a safe and nonviolent working environment for the teaching and ancillary staff, but also protect the young people for whose well-being and care they are ultimately responsible. It is a complex problem, and one to which I would contribute the following thoughts:

- A school is a workplace. But imagine it as a workplace in which students are the employees, and teaching staff are the management. Payment is granted to the students in the form of education, and to the teachers, in the form of the usual paycheck. Your school should operate just like any other workplace, with policies and procedures in place to protect the rights of both the employees and the leaders.
- This being the case, there must be a Code of Conduct for all. This code can be negotiated with the student council, and adopted as a norm for the entire school community. The code states explicitly what is

acceptable behavior and what is not. Each person in the school has to sign off every year on reading and accepting its terms.

- The Code of Conduct is supplemented by a "zero tolerance for violence" policy and procedure, again applicable to all in the school community. The policy defines violence in the context of a school environment, indicates the complaint procedure and outlines the sanctions applicable for infringements, up to and including expulsion.

- A crisis management team should also be in place to respond to incidents. This team can also have representation from the parent-teacher association and school volunteers.

- It might be worth considering a student assistance program, through which students have access to confidential counseling suitable for their age group and maturity level. Two considerations, of course, would be a) the cost involved and b) parental consent for those too young to make the decision to obtain counseling.

School boards also should be collaborating to develop policies and standards of good practice for addressing the problem of the raging student, taking into account the boundaries and limitations imposed by ethics and law. There should not be an assumption that a teacher, merely by being a teacher, is well-equipped to deal with anger and conflict. Opportunities for training in dealing with the difficult student, or, for that matter, the difficult parent, should be made available.

Religious Communities

Religion, one of the means by which many of us find peace and serenity in life, can at the same time incite people to violence. One of the greatest gifts we have as citizens who live in a democracy is the ability to speak freely, and heaven forbid that this should ever change. But coupled with freedom of speech is the freedom to condemn. All too often today, religious leaders use their right to freedom of speech as permission to take an open pulpit, and promote hatred, homophobia, racism, sexism and all other kinds of bigotry. The condemnatory remarks that are directed to mass audiences encourage hatred, fear, ignorance and intolerance. It's disquieting to find religious leaders throwing stones at the face of equality, respect for the person and dignity of the individual. Their condemnatory remarks are always directed to the "objective" group, but they forget, it seems, that the group comprises sentient individuals. Society is not, as I have said before, some kind of globular entity, but is made up of individuals, each of whom is worthy of respect and dignity as a human being.

Religion is always a difficult topic to mention in any piece of writing, since so many people have so much vested interest in their own religious beliefs and practices. I do have a certain distinct point of view regarding religious matters, having been for a number of years one of those "religious leaders." But when I observe the world and recognize the vast chasms that separate people because of religious differences, I can't help but wonder why current religious leaders do not make more of an effort to condemn violence. I have to question why the anti-abortionists are becoming murderers themselves. I have to question the Holy War theory! I cannot let myself think or accept that ethnic cleansing is a result of belief in the goodness of the one, true God! These are just a few of the many larger issues that abound, and I wonder how much influence these religious agendas have on the way people really think about each other in the workplace.

I think religious leaders have a duty to uphold all that is good, true and just. And they have a responsibility to condemn violence, whether in the workplace or anywhere else. People do take their religion, attitudes and beliefs to work.

The Legal System

At some point the legislators have to exert influence. It would be preferable if organizations made voluntary provisions to introduce policies and procedures around zero tolerance at work. However, some organizations would wait until they were pushed into action by legislation. And some would wait until they faced a violent crisis at work before taking steps to protect their businesses, their staff and themselves.

I would like to see all Canadians having the same protection in law. This is not currently the case. If you happen to live in British Columbia, Saskatchewan or Nova Scotia, you have a certain equality in law by way of protection from workplace violence. In these provinces, if your work is considered to be at risk of violence, then your employer must inform you, must provide security to minimize your risks, and, in the event of an incident, is obliged to provide appropriate supports. The legislation will also cover you for injury associated with a violent event, including psychological injury.

If you happen to reside in the other provinces or territories, the situation is slightly different. There may well be provision in the Workers' Compensation Board rules (or Workplace Safety and Insurance Board in Ontario) for injury resulting from violence, and there may be some provision from the Criminal Injuries Compensation Board, but regions differ considerably. I would make the following recommendations:

- There should be a federal approach to the problem of work rage.
- This approach should provide equitable measures in law to minimize the risks to the employee from violence.
- It should clearly provide for the introduction of appropriate security wherever possible.
- It has to have the power to force organizations to maintain adequate supports, both financial and psychological, for those affected by a violent incident.

The Political System

This is the post–Cold War era. The Berlin Wall came tumbling down 10 years ago. The demobilization and dismantling of the intercontinental ballistic missiles continues. A new era of peace reigns! Meanwhile, half of the former USSR is starving, and the other half is fighting. China still persecutes free thinkers. South Africa is now a country free from apartheid, but one where reverse apartheid is a distinct possibility. In the Middle East, there may soon be a peace agreement between the Israelis and the Palestinians, but in the meantime the fighting, the bombing and the dislocation proceed. For Northern Ireland, peace has been agreed to on paper, but no one wants to disarm. The new era of peace is not so peaceful.

The world of politics is a violent one, and it influences us every breathing moment. Personally, I think I should be a child of the future—the *Star Trek* future—where illness and disease have ended, where money matters no more, and where people live in Skinnerian behavioral bliss! But then I come back down to Earth with a *bang*. Even ardent Trekkies would have to agree that while captains Kirk, Picard, Sisko and Janeway may have helped to eradicate illness and disease, they did not manage to eradicate rage and war!

The eradication of rage, and in particular work rage, will take political determination. And since rage, or at the very least anger, seems to be a human predisposition, it will take generations of humans with political determination to effect major change. Politics influences us, and we, too, can influence politicians. Eliminating the danger of workplace rage will require the support of a large number of challengers, beginning with you and me.

The Organization

The challenge in preventing and responding to work rage will be greatest for organizations. We have already seen that work rage is a problem that goes beyond the Canadian and U.S. workplace; it transcends geographical boundaries. However, many trends in business operations are set here in North America, so the impetus for change may well be here, too.

Recent studies indicate ever-increasing levels of stress-related illnesses induced by high organizational expectations and demands on individual time and energy. We have listened for years to the theorists who say that more and more of our time will be devoted to recreational pursuits because of the advances in technology. Is this happening? Absolutely not! During the 1990s, people have worked harder and longer, and devoted less time to home and family, not to mention recreation. In my wanderings throughout Canada, I have heard one constant complaint from employees in all types of organizations: there is too much work to do. And the employers' expectation is that people are going to keep doing the work.

Some organizations must have the courage to deliver a definitive and loud "No!" when shareholders demand more return on their investment. Of course, organizations can be trimmed to be more efficient and effective, but the greater return to the shareholders in profit dividends comes at a cost: tired, overworked, unmotivated employees.

Employer expectations must be realistic. Most people work to live, rather than live to work. And there is a limit to the amount of dedication most employees can feel for their work. It is when people become tired and stressed that the tolerance level for maltreatment diminishes. The organization has to be aware that it may bring on a violent episode through excessive demands on employee time and effort.

This provides a huge challenge, then, to the organization in its corporate entity, and to those in leadership who set the pace for output, efficiency and profitability. The organizational answer to this challenge is generally something like "If you can't take the heat, get out of the kitchen." In other words, the rat race is here, and it is here to stay—if you don't like it, move on. But only a minuscule percentage of the population is actually able to leave the rat race behind, retire to the pine forests of British Columbia and live happily ever after. The opportunity to move on is restricted, and for many reasons.

Our society as a whole abhors the notion of slave labor. When it comes to light that some celebrity-endorsed product or garment is produced at ridiculously low cost in a sweatshop in some developing part of the world, there is a huge outcry. And rightly so. Yet no one really seems to pay heed to any of the national statistics that point to the fact that workers in Canada today experience a high degree of stress. It is time for a reevaluation of organizational ethics and work practices in order to restore a sense of balance to our work and home life.

Radical thinking is not my forte. In fact, politics has never been high on my personal agenda. I would much rather take myself off to the movies than listen to political exhortations on poverty, disease and homelessness. Shameful, perhaps, since I should have the interests of others in proper perspective. However, as I grow toward greater maturity, I realize that my opinions do become more refined—and more cynical!

I have witnessed the same kind of cynicism across the country. Perhaps it is part of the typical Canadian attitude, or maybe it is endemic to the developed world. In any case, it is certainly "in the air," and particularly in the world of organizational behavior. It contributes to the restlessness found in the workplace today, and probably adds to the growing problem of work rage.

Perhaps we will, in fact, reach year 2010 with a sense of achievement, seeing more tolerance, less frustration, and a workplace free from the effects of excessive stress. But if so, there's a lot to be done between now and then!

Chapter 17

Rage: What Are *You* Going to Do?

"What are you going to do about violence?" asked my old friend Eddie. And so it began.

Work Rage has taken both you, the reader, and me on a journey, reflecting on the past, observing the current state of rage in the workplace, and making recommendations for the future. As stated in the Introduction, this work was never intended to be an academic treatise on violence. Though I can't stop myself from philosophizing occasionally, I do not pretend to be an academic. In my writing, I am aware, I speak from the heart, and sometimes in a way that sounds condemnatory of many of the wonderful institutions, organizations and associations I have been privileged to work with over the past 20 years. If so, it is because I sincerely believe in what I do.

In *Work Rage*, I have shared many details of my own involvement in post-violence "mop-up." The anecdotes throughout are recounted truthfully, though the names have been changed. Those in Scotland who know my past well will be able to piece together the jigsaw puzzle and reach their own conclusions about certain events—and they are welcome to do so.

In writing *Work Rage*, it was my intention to share with readers my reflections and opinions on workplace violence, based on my own deep involvement with trauma response. Many readers will not share these opinions; in fact, they will probably be outraged, especially by my observations around management style and practice in Canada. This may be destined to create controversy—and I sincerely hope it does! I do think the time has come for a realistic evaluation of the role that work itself plays in today's faster-moving, multitasking, highly stressing and more aggressive workplace. Does the modern work environment itself exacerbate the problem of work rage? I think it does.

My appetite for research on and experience in work rage trauma response has developed into a sort of gluttony. I never seem to be able to do enough, and, as far as I can see, there is so much yet to do to address this growing problem. I look forward to the day when it is no longer necessary for people like myself—and all the other wonderful people in this country who respond to violent trauma—to offer help and support after violence.

Meanwhile, I offer the reader this book, *Work Rage*, in the hope that you will find some useful information or advice to help you in your quest to address the problem. Most of you will never be faced with having to handle an employee or co-worker who brings a baseball bat to work, thank goodness. But even if the ideas in this book give you the confidence to stand up and say to a verbally abusive colleague, "Your behavior is not acceptable!" that, too, is great.

If this publication is in any way able to influence one person to provide protection to employees from the effects of work rage, then my own quest to do something about violence, planted in my thoughts all those years ago by my friend Eddie, will be fulfilled.